Language Understanding

Open Guides to Psychology

Series Editor: Judith Greene, Professor of Psychology at the Open University

Titles in the series

Learning to Use Statistical Tests in Psychology
Judith Greene and Manuela D'Oliveira

Basic Cognitive Processes
Judith Greene and Carolyn Hicks

Memory: A Cognitive Approach
Gillian Cohen, Michael W. Eysenck and Martin E. Le Voi

Language Understanding: A Cognitive Approach
Judith Greene

Problem Solving: A Cognitive Approach
Hank Kahney

Perception and Representation: A Cognitive Approach
Ilona Roth and John Frisby

Titles in preparation

Designing and Reporting Experiments
Peter Harris

Issues in Brain and Behaviour
Frederick Toates

Basic Social Psychology
Dorothy Miell

Language Understanding:
A Cognitive Approach

Judith Greene

Open University Press
Milton Keynes · Philadelphia

Open University Press
Open University Educational Enterprises Limited
12 Cofferidge Close
Stony Stratford
Milton Keynes MK11 1BY, England
and
242 Cherry Street
Philadelphia, PA 19106, USA

First published 1986

British Library Cataloguing in Publication Data

Greene, Judith   Language Understanding: A Cognitive Approach. —
    (Open Guides to Psychology)
    1. Cognition   2. Psycholinguistics
    1. Title   2. Open University
    153.4   BF311

ISBN 0–335–15326–7

Library of Congress Cataloging in Publication Data

Greene, Judith.
    Language Understanding.
    Bibliography: P.
    Includes indexes.
    1. Psycholinguistics.   2. Cognition.   3. Competence
    and performance (linguistics) 1. Title, DNLM:
    1. Cognition.   2.Language   3.Psycholinguistics.
    BF 455   GS11L
    BF 455.G737   1985   401'9   85-21582

ISBN 0–335–15326–7

Typeset by Marlborough Design, Oxford
Printed in Great Britain at the Alden Press, Oxford

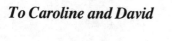

To Caroline and David

Language Understanding: A Cognitive Approach

Contents

Overview   141

Preface

Within the Open Guides to Psychology series *Language Understanding: A Cognitive Approach* is one of a companion set of four books, the others covering *Memory*, *Problem Solving*, and *Perception and Representation*. Together these form the main texts of the Open University third level course in Cognitive Psychology, but each of the four volumes can be read on its own. The course is designed for second or third year students. It is presented in the style and format that the Open University has found to be uniquely effective in making the material intelligible and interesting.

The books provide an up-to-date in-depth treatment of the major issues, theories and findings in cognitive psychology. They are designed to introduce a representative selection of different research methods, and the reader is encouraged, by means of Activities and Self-assessment Questions interpolated through the text, to become involved in cognitive psychology as an active participant.

The author gratefully acknowledges the many helpful comments and suggestions of fellow members of the course team on earlier drafts, and the valuable assistance of Pat Vasiliou in typing the manuscript.

Introduction

This book is divided into three parts, each of which introduces a different approach to language understanding. Part I emphasizes the enormous amount of knowledge required to explain our ability to understand what we hear and read. To start with, we have to know the vocabulary and grammar of a language. But, as you have probably realized if you have ever tried to learn a foreign language, much more is required in order to be able to communicate effectively. Apart from many idiomatic phrases, a speaker has to know the social conventions for language use. Finally, if you know nothing about the topic under discussion, you are not likely to understand much about what is being said.

Part II focuses on the various types of representations and processes which underlie language use. These range from word definitions and grammatical rules to the processes involved in understanding a whole text, story or newspaper article. One point which emerges is that different sources of knowledge interact in language processing. Rather than simply building up interpretations from the bottom-up, starting with words and sentences and working up to texts, we bring to bear all sorts of expectations which determine how we are likely to interpret language.

In Part III, several models of language understanding are introduced which are implemented as computer programs. Not surprisingly, in view of the many processes involved in language understanding, computer programs have not so far been developed to simulate all aspects of human language. In general, they have dealt with restricted domains, which only need a small vocabulary, fairly simple grammatical constructions and, most importantly, a limited amount of general knowledge. Nevertheless, because of the need to specify precise program instructions, these computer models have drawn attention to many subtle characteristics of human language.

Finally, the Overview reiterates one of the main themes of this book, the interaction between different types of knowledge in language processing. Because of the emphasis on knowledge, this book inevitably deals with theories about how linguistic and general knowledge are stored in memory. Consequently, this volume is complementary to the *Memory* volume in the Open Guides to Psychology series.

Perhaps I should end this introduction by stating which areas of language understanding will *not* be covered in this book. There will be nothing about how speech sounds are analysed or how individual letters are recognized as words. Important as these problems are for theories of speech perception and reading, they would require another book to deal with them adequately. In this volume the language understanding process is taken as starting at the point when language users have recognized spoken or written words. The problem of how they attribute meanings to individual words, sentences and texts raises complex representational issues which are of special relevance to cognitive psychology.

How to use this guide

In each section of this book you will find Self-Assessment Questions (SAQs) inserted at various points in the text. Attempting all the SAQs should give you a better understanding of theoretical issues and research techniques. They will also help to make you an active participant instead of just a passive reader. The answers can be found at the end of the book and will help to illuminate points made in the text.

Detailed accounts of experiments are presented in Techniques Boxes; these are chosen to illustrate commonly used experimental methods. The Summaries at the end of each section recapitulate the main points and so provide a useful aid to revision. The Index of Concepts that appears at the end of the book indicates the place in the text where each concept is first introduced and defined. Entries in the Index of Concepts are italicized in the text.

At the end of each part of the book there is a short list of recommended further reading. Obviously the interested reader can also follow up other references given in the text. Some of these references are to articles in the Open University Reader *Issues in Modeling Cognition*, edited by Aitkenhead and Slack. This is designed to be a companion volume to the other cognitive psychology volumes in the Open Guides to Psychology series.

Part I
Language and Knowledge

Judith Greene

Contents

1   Introduction

All psychology textbooks start chapters on language with an introduction pointing out the crucial importance of language in human affairs. There is no doubt that most of us talk a lot. Even people who lead relatively solitary lives are exposed to language via TV, radio, books and newspapers. What is the point of all this chatter?

Conventionally, language is defined as having two main functions: external communications with other people and internal representations of our own thoughts. The advent of writing has resulted in so many written records that years of education are now deemed necessary for children to learn the accumulated history and scientific discoveries of their culture, the 'thinking' of past generations. It is difficult to conceive how any civilisation could exist without developing some method for communicating thoughts.

In the light of this, it may seem a trivial matter to define language and communication. You may be surprised to hear that whole books have been written to try to answer the questions 'what is language?' and 'what is communication?'.

The problem is that these terms can be used in so many ways. 'Language separates man from animals' refers to language as an ability which is universal to all humans. 'English is a rich and flexible language' refers to one of the many human languages, the one which happens to be spoken by members of English-speaking societies and by many other people as a second language. 'The English language is derived from Latin and Anglo-Saxon roots' suggests that a language 'exists' as an entity in its own right with a history of change over the centuries. 'John knows English' refers to language as part of an individual's knowledge. 'John speaks English well' implies that there can be variations in the way individuals use a generally accepted language. 'John said he was going home' is a particular utterance which can be understood by any speaker of the English language. 'John's home is over there' is an utterance which will only communicate something in a context in which it is obvious what 'over there' means. 'It's chilly' can be interpreted as a comment about the weather or as a request to close the window. A shrug of the shoulders may communicate disinterest.

I am certainly not going to try to sort out all the terminological issues which have puzzled philosophers and linguists for hundreds of years. There is, however, one important distinction you should bear in mind. This is a contrast which has often been made between competence and performance. *Competence* refers to people's knowledge of a language, the knowledge that enables them to produce and understand utterances in that language. *Performance* refers to the production and comprehension of utterances, whether in speech or writing. Any faults or hesitations in speech or writing are thought to be due to temporary lapses which affect performance but do not necessarily reflect on people's underlying competence.

The idea behind this distinction is that people 'know' the vocabulary and grammatical rules of any language they can speak. This represents their competence in that language. In performance speakers may hesitate, make grammatical errors or repeat themselves; listeners may misinterpret what is said to them. Competence is sometimes described as a speaker's 'ideal' knowledge of language. This is contrasted with performance factors, such as forgetting what one meant to say, which may affect the production and comprehension of individual utterances.

The competence/performance distinction neatly divides language between two academic disciplines. *Linguistics* is the study of languages as linguistic systems. Linguists describe the phonetic sound patterns, grammars and vocabularies of languages. (In this context linguists are academics who study linguistics – not necessarily fluent speakers of several languages.) It was a well-known linguist Noam Chomsky (1965) who crystallized the competence/performance distinction. Modern linguists claim to be describing the competence underlying normal language usage, rather than prescribing what constitutes 'good grammar'. Nevertheless, they are looking for grammatical rules which will explain our ability to recognize and produce correct sentences, i.e. linguistic competence. From this point of view, slips of the tongue or spelling errors can be considered irrelevant, if not positively misleading.

A diametrically opposed view is that it is language use which is all important. Psychologists are naturally interested in the performance factors which affect the way people actually use language. Even within linguistics there are researchers known as *sociolinguists* because of their interest in the social functions of language. They observe how people tailor their speech, and use nonverbal signals, to convey meanings appropriate to the social situation and the social status of the speakers and listeners.

Cognitive psychology sits somewhat uneasily between these two extremes. Cognitive psychologists are concerned with mental representations; so they, like the linguists, are interested in how the knowledge underlying language use is represented in the mind. They are equally committed to investigating the mental processes which are responsible for the production and understanding of individual utterances appropriate to the context in which they occur.

For this reason, psychologists have questioned whether it makes sense to separate knowledge of linguistic rules (competence) from language use (performance). Instead of isolating an 'idealized' grammatical competence from an error-prone performance, the aim of cognitive psychology is to describe all the knowledge which is responsible for language behaviour, including the processes involved in the production and understanding of apparently ungrammatical utterances.

SAQ 1
John's if he gets here in time.
(a) Is this sentence grammatical?
(b) Try to think of a question to which this reply would make sense in a conversational context.

The implication is that linguistic competence should include, not only the grammar and vocabulary of a language, but also the ability to select from among a myriad of possible utterances only those which convey appropriate meanings. On top of all this, we are usually very good at choosing just the right 'style' for our communications, formal for formal occasions, chatty with our friends, plain and clear, I hope, in textbooks like this one.

This wider definition of linguistic competence to encompass selection of communicative utterances has been called *communicative competence*, to distinguish it from purely linguistic competence. As we shall see in later sections, extending the aims of cognitive pyschologists who study language to cover communicative competence only makes the task of studying knowledge representations and language processing harder than ever.

Summary of Section 1

- The term 'language' can be used to refer to:
  (a) A universal human ability.
  (b) A particular language understood by one or more communities of language speakers.
  (c) The fact that an individual knows a particular language.
  (d) The use of utterances to communicate in particular contexts.
- Linguistic competence refers to the linguistic knowledge which enables speakers to produce and understand sentences. Linguists study the linguistic rules of phonetics, grammar and vocabulary which constitute the 'ideal' competence of language speakers.
- Linguistic performance refers to the production and understanding of particular utterances, which may include slips, errors and

misunderstandings. Psychologists and sociolinguists are interested in the factors which influence the selection of meaningful communications in social contexts.

- Cognitive psychologists who study language are interested in the knowledge representations involved in all aspects of language use, including the ability to communicate and understand meanings (communicative competence).

2   Types of linguistic knowledge

Now that we have cleared the air, how do we go about finding out what kind of knowledge representations are needed for language use? Just to convince you that there is something here which needs explaining, consider an imaginary tribe called the Shivasi, who live in the desert, hoard every drop of water and worship water spirits. Can you understand the following sentence in the Shivasi language? *Psiht Shivasi gor brok me Babwe fyp.* No, of course you can't. But all members of the Shivasi tribe can! So what does one need to know about a language in order to understand it?

2.1   Lexical meanings and syntax

Sometimes the writing system of a language may be unfamiliar: for instance, the text might be in Russian, Persian or Hebrew script. Luckily the Shivasi language uses 'English' letters. So the first thing you might want to ask is what each of the individual words means. Suppose I tell you that in Shivasi *psiht* means 'look'; *Shivasi* means 'Shivasi'; *gor* means 'water'; *brok* means 'then'; *me* means 'not'; *Babwe* means 'Babwe'; *fyp* means 'run'. Are you any wiser about what *Look Shivasi water then not Babwe run* means? The meanings of words are termed *lexical meanings* (from *lexicon*, which is another word for a dictionary). What is obvious from the above example is that knowing the lexical meanings of words is not necessarily sufficient to elucidate the meaning of a whole utterance.

The next question to consider is how individual words are combined into meaningful utterances. *Syntax* is the technical term for what you probably think of as the grammar of a language. Syntax includes rules for combining words in certain orders and adding appropriate *inflections* (i.e. adding endings to words such as *ed* to indicate the past tense, or *s* to form plurals).

It may seem quite a simple matter to formulate the syntactic rules for a language. But imagine trying to explain to a foreigner why it is possible to say, *Are you coming or aren't you?* but not *Am I coming or amn't I?*. Why is it grammatical to say *He walked in* but not *He camed in*; *two houses* but not *two mouses*? And, of course, there are hundreds of similar cases. If you have ever tried to explain examples like these, you will appreciate the task of a linguist attempting to formalize all the rules which are required to produce grammatically correct English sentences.

In the Shivasi sentence, for instance, you would have to know that the form of the word *Shivasi* indicates that it is the subject of the sentence. Used as an adjective in the phrase *a Shivasi tent*, the word would have a different ending, *Shivasia*. You would have to know that the first and last words of a sentence always make up the main verb; also that *then not* refers to the present time because the Shivasi language always refers to the past unless it is specifically denied. So now you know that the sentence has the following grammatical structure: *Shivasi* (subject) *look/run* (main verb) *then not* (present tense) *water Babwe*. But you may still be puzzled about what the sentence really means.

2.2   Semantics and general knowledge

All members of the Shivasi tribe know that *Babwe* is the name of a forest; and that *look run water* means 'explore' (because of their obsession about water!). And there is no need to specify how many Shivasi there are because they never go exploring except in a group of at least thirty people. So a fluent speaker of Shivasi would immediately understand that the sentence means 'At least thirty of my people are at present exploring the Babwe forest'. The analysis of the meanings of utterances is known as *semantics* (semantics is simply another term for the study of meanings).

You may be thinking that the Shivasi sentence is an exaggerated example. But what would a Shivasi make of the English sentence: *Visiting aunts can be a nuisance?*

SAQ 2
(a) Did you notice that the 'aunts' sentence has two quite different meanings?
(b) If the Shivasi had a custom which forbade them to visit female relatives, which meaning would they be likely to select?
(c) What if female relatives always had to stay at home?

All these examples demonstrate the importance of knowledge about social contexts in determining the meanings of utterances. Indeed one problem is that the general knowledge needed to interpret the meanings of utterances is potentially unlimited. The two meanings of the sentence *Visiting aunts can be a nuisance* may be semantically comprehensible to any English speaker. However, in a society in which aunts were always respected and loved, neither meaning of the 'visiting aunts' sentence would be acceptable as a communicative statement.

A visiting linguist might learn from his investigations of the Shivasi language that *Shivasi* is the plural form of a noun, but he would need to be an anthropologist to discover that the Shivasi never go exploring except in groups of thirty. When I see on a poster 'The Police live at the Albert Hall', how do I understand this to mean that a pop group will be performing in person, rather than that members of the constabulary inhabit that vast building?

The point about these examples is that they raise the issue of whether all our 'real-life' knowledge about aunts and what goes on at the Albert Hall should be included in our linguistic knowledge of the English language. The relationship between purely linguistic knowledge of a language and general knowledge about the world remains one of the most problematic issues in cognitive theories of language.

2.3   Language use and pragmatics

So far we have been talking as if meanings can be allocated to individual sentences regardless of the linguistic context in which they are used. But the Shivasi sentence might have been part of a long story about the Shivasi exploring the forest in search of a lost girl. This would set up expectations about how succeeding sentences should be interpreted, e.g. *She had wandered far*. Analysis of the *linguistic context* in which a sentence is embedded is called *textual linguistics* or *discourse analysis*.

Sentences in isolation are often ambiguous and require a linguistic context to disambiguate them. Even a very simple sentence like *He gave her a ring* may be given a different interpretation depending on whether it occurs in the linguistic context of *John asked Mary to marry him* or *John wanted to talk to Mary*. There are many other utterances which only make sense if both participants are aware of the same situation. For example, *Put it next to the big one* can only be understood if the listener can see the objects being discussed; this is sometimes termed *situational context*.

Finally, there is the use of language in a *social context*. When people use language in a face-to-face situation they are usually trying to achieve some aim, such as persuading, showing off, or requesting information. This level of analysis is sometimes called *pragmatics* because it takes into account the purpose of language in achieving pragmatic ends. The use of language to perform particular functions has also been analysed as *speech acts* (Searle, 1970). The speech act of 'requesting' (e.g. to get someone to close a window) may be expressed as a question, *Will you close the window?*, a statement, *It's chilly in here*, or as a direct command, *Close that window*. The way people interpret these utterances depends on their appreciation of a speaker's intentions.

To end with an example from our – totally imaginary – Shivasi tribe, a speaker might have chosen a slightly different phraseology to refer to the exploration of the Babwe forest depending on whether it was in reply to a query from his chief about how many people were left in the village to take part in a ceremony, as opposed to telling a close friend it was too late for him to join the exploring party.

Most examples of language use involve some form of interaction, either face-to-face or between writers and readers. Utterances are never produced in a vacuum but are embedded in a linguistic, situational or social context.

2.4   *Knowledge representations*

From what I have said so far it is obvious that as language speakers we must have competence in the vocabulary and syntax of our language. In addition, we need to know a lot about the world and the conventions for acceptable communications in our society. Without this, we may be able to produce correct grammatical sentences but fail to communicate what we mean to other speakers or to the readers of our written communications.

For cognitive psychologists these issues can be rephrased as asking how such knowledge is represented in memory. Is our knowledge of grammatical rules represented as a special syntactic component in memory? Is our dictionary of lexical meanings separate from our general knowledge of the world to which they refer? Do we, for instance, store the meaning of the word 'tree' as a tall plant separately from our general knowledge about trees? How is our knowledge about social conventions organized so as to constrain our utterances to make sense?

What we are really talking about here is the whole of human memory. In order to narrow down the problem to manageable proportions, the knowledge required for language use has been

23

broken down into several topics which have tended to be studied in isolation from each other. In the remaining sections of Part 1 we shall be considering the role of general knowledge in language understanding.

Summary of Section 2

- Traditionally the types of knowledge required for language understanding have been divided into the following categories:
  - (a) Lexical meanings: meanings of words listed in a lexicon (dictionary).
  - (b) Syntax: grammatical rules for combining words in sentences, including word order and word endings (inflections).
  - (c) Semantics: rules for combining word meanings into meaningful sentences.
  - (d) Discourse analysis: analysis of linguistic context.
  - (e) Pragmatics: the use of language to communicate intentions by speech acts in social contexts.
- All these types of knowledge are stored as mental representations in memory.

3   Inferences in language comprehension

Let me start by reminding you that in the previous section there were several demonstrations of the fact that there is more to language understanding than the literal meanings of the words in a sentence. The language user has to 'go beyond' the literal meaning of utterances in order to understand the intentions of the speaker and the likely meanings of an utterance in a particular context. This 'going beyond' the input is what is known in psychology as making an *inference*.

Psychologists have often pointed out that it is a general characteristic of humans to make inferences in order to make sense of everything they see or hear. To take just one example, most of you must have had the experience of glancing at a newspaper headline and immediately starting to work out what it must be referring to. Just this morning I saw the headline ENGLAND'S TALL ORDER. Its being on the sport page started me off making inferences about possible sporting references, 'tall' made me think of basketball – but it turned out to be a problem for the English netball team of how to win against an extremely tall Jamaican player. By the way, did the mention of netball encourage you to make the inference that I was referring to a tall *woman*? In that case, how tall is 'tall' likely to be?

I hope you are now convinced that making inferences about what utterances refer to is part of the normal interpretation of linguistic inputs. For instance, as long as I can speak idiomatic English, I can understand the headline ENGLAND'S TALL ORDER as meaning that 'England' is facing some sort of difficult task, or possibly has ordered something tall. But I had to make a lot of inferences to ascertain the actual situation the headline was referring to. One problem with studying the inferences involved in understanding utterances is that inferences of this kind are so instantaneous that we are often only aware of making them when we are faced with a really ambiguous linguistic input.

3.1   The given-new contract

One way of analysing what sentences are meant to refer to is to divide each utterance into *given information* and *new information*. The purpose of a speaker is to convey a piece of 'new' information, but to do this it is essential that the listener knows what the new information is referring to. If the listener does not know the reference of an utterance, the new information will not make much sense.

Normally it is assumed that both speaker and hearer share information about the topic of conversation; in other words, the reference is already known, or 'given'. For instance, if someone says *She left to go home*, without any indication of who 'she' is, I might very well reply *Who on earth are you talking about?*. The speaker mistakenly thinks that I already know the information which is assumed to be given.

Clark (1977) pointed out that speakers often select utterances so as to make it obvious to the listener what is assumed to be given information and what is new. The sentence *Mary left the party to go home* implies that 'Mary' is the given information to which the new information that she left to go home is being added. The sentence *It was Mary who left the party early* implies that the given information is that 'someone left the party early' and the new information is that it was Mary who did so.

SAQ 3
Indicate the given and the new information in the following sentences:
(a) *Peter was the one who broke the window.*
(b) *Peter was kicking a ball around when he broke the window.*

Clark (1977) also introduced the idea of a *given-new contract* which holds between a speaker and a listener, or a writer and reader. According to the contract, it is the duty of a speaker or writer to indicate the given information by making it clear who or what is being referred to. An example would be to say *Mary Brown was feeling ill; so she left to go home.* Sometimes it is not necessary to spell things out as explicitly as this, since the speaker may correctly assume that the listener already knows the given information. For instance, if both the speaker and listener had actually witnessed Mary looking ill at a party, the speaker could just say *She's left to go home.*

Clark gives some examples when the speaker's indication of given information is more indirect, as in the sentences *I walked into John's room. The chandeliers sparkled brightly.* In this case the inference has to be made that the chandeliers are hanging in the room the speaker walked into. Clark calls this a *bridging inference* because it 'goes beyond' the literal meaning of sentences in order to make a 'bridge' between what was actually said and the inference that the second sentence referred to the chandeliers in John's room. If the speaker had meant to refer to some other chandeliers, he would have had to make this clear.

What is the role of the listener in the given-new contract? The listener has to act on the assumption that the speaker is attempting to provide the appropriate information on which to base plausible bridging inferences. In the above example, the listener could have said 'what chandeliers?' instead of making the bridging inference that the speaker must have meant the ones in John's room.

Other examples of bridging inferences rely on the listener making plausible inferences about likely results and causes of events. For instance, hearing the sentences *John was murdered yesterday. The knife lay nearby*, most people would infer that John had been stabbed to death.

SAQ 4
I ran two miles. It did me good.
  What bridging inference has to be made to identify what the pronoun 'it' is referring to?

Clark and Murphy (1982) have extended the notion of the given-new contract by introducing the more general term *audience design*. This refers to the fact that we always intend our utterances to be understood by the particular audience to whom they are addressed. Utterances are never meant to be understood in isolation. Understanding is always based on the assumption that speaker and listener share some mutual knowledge and beliefs.

The fact that listeners make the assumption that a speaker must have good reason to expect them to understand on the basis of shared knowledge is known as the *design assumption*. It is this assumption which leads listeners to make bridging inferences in order to understand the meanings and reference of utterances.

3.2   Bridging inferences

Most linguistic communications proceed smoothly without our even noticing any bridging inferences we may be making. A good conversationalist makes sure that a listener has, or can reasonably be expected to infer, the required given information. Remarks which introduce a new topic are often prefaced by statements like *You know the old house we saw last week*. Often the topic is obvious, particularly between close friends. Writing a letter to a friend will be very different from writing for an unknown audience of readers. Skilled writers take care to remove potential ambiguities in their prose, avoiding sentence constructions which could be interpreted in more than one way. Sometimes things go wrong in spite of all our efforts. A nice example is given by Parsons (1969):

> Completing an impressive ceremony, the Admiral's lovely daughter smashed a bottle over her stern as she slid gracefully down the slipways.

Because of our tendency to make bridging inferences about what situation is being described, the writer – and probably many of his readers – simply didn't notice the ambiguity of the possible references for the pronouns 'her' and 'she'.

Bridging inferences are ubiquitous in language understanding. Clark claims that listeners can only understand sentences if they already have in mind an *antecedent* for the given information, or can construct an antecedent by making a bridging inference. Listeners will only be able to understand the sentence *She left to go home* if they can create an antecedent for 'she' by making the inference that it must be referring to someone already known or recently mentioned. Clark and his colleagues carried out experiments to test the notion of bridging inferences, an example of which is described in Techniques Box A overleaf.

Clark's theory is concerned with the way people go about identifying given information in order to understand a sentence. Of course, it all depends on what you mean by understanding a sentence. In one sense, any English speaker can understand the literal meaning of the sentence *The beer was warm* without having the faintest notion what beer is being referred to. However, Clark's definition of language understanding emphasizes the fact that all utterances are intended to be understood by a particular audience in a particular context.

TECHNIQUES BOX A

Haviland and Clark's Experiment (1974)

Rationale
Haviland and Clark predicted that sentences which require bridging inferences will take longer to read than sentences in which the antecedent for the given information has been directly referred to. They used pairs of sentences like (a) and (b):
(a) *George got some beer out of the car. The beer was warm.*
(b) *Andrew was especially fond of beer. The beer was warm.*
They argue that (a) is an example of a Direct Antecedent because the first sentence directly refers to 'the beer' which is the given information referred to as being warm in the second sentence. The pair of sentences in (b) is an example of an Indirect Antecedent because the fact that Andrew likes beer in general does not provide an exact referent for the particular beer which is being referred to as warm. The listener has to make a bridging inference that Andrew brought some of his favourite beer along on this occasion.

Method
Subjects (i.e. the people taking part in the experiment) were presented with pairs of sentences like (a) or (b) on a screen. They were asked to press a button as soon as they felt they had understood the second sentence. The times subjects took to press the button were recorded.

Results
The average time subjects took to press the button for Direct Antecedent pairs was 1,031 milliseconds and for Indirect Antecedent pairs, 1,168 milliseconds. This finding supports Haviland and Clark's hypothesis that comprehension takes longer when bridging inferences have to be constructed in order to identify the antecedent for the given information in the second sentence.

Sometimes, of course, bridging inferences intended by the speaker are not the same as those assumed by the listener. Take the sentence: *John was dancing with Susan when Mary left the party early*. This would be easy to understand if both speaker and hearer know the past history of the three characters. Even an outsider might infer that Mary was John's wife or girlfriend. But sometimes a listener may jump to the wrong conclusions. The speaker might have meant to imply that Mary decided to leave the party because she disapproved of dancing, or simply had a headache. The inference that Mary might be annoyed by John choosing to dance with Susan is based on a stereotype of male/female relationships. Understanding depends on shared assumptions about social conventions. Misunderstandings arise when the design assumption of mutual knowledge and beliefs breaks down.

3.3   Inferences and memory

Another methodological technique for demonstrating that people make inferences is to test their memory for sentences and stories. The basic notion is that, rather than remembering the exact *verbatim* wording of utterances and texts, people remember meanings. If they make inferences in order to make sense of utterances, they will be likely to remember information they have inferred as well as information which was explicitly mentioned in a text.

Bransford and his colleagues carried out a series of experiments to explore the role of inferences in language understanding by testing whether subjects can later pick out (i.e. recognize) sentences they have actually heard from other sentences which describe possible inferences, a technique known as *recognition confusions*. A typical experiment is described in Techniques Box B.

TECHNIQUES BOX B

Bransford, Barclay and Franks's Recognition Experiment (1972)

Rationale
If people make inferences while they are listening to sentences, when they are later asked to recognize a particular sentence they will not be sure whether it is one of the original sentences or whether it is a new sentence which expresses a probable inference they might have made when listening to the sentences.

Method
For one group of subjects, sentences like (a) were read aloud, while another group of subjects heard sentences like (b):
(a) *Three turtles rested beside a floating log and a fish swam beneath them.*
(b) *Three turtles rested on a floating log and a fish swam beneath them.*
Check for yourself that in (b), but not in (a), it is possible to infer that the fish swam underneath the log on which the turtles were resting.

> Subjects were later presented with a list of sentences and asked to pick out (i.e. recognize) the 'old' sentences they had originally heard from other sentences like (c) and (d):
>
> (c) *Three turtles rested beside a floating log and a fish swam beneath it.*
>
> (d) *Three turtles rested on a floating log and a fish swam beneath it.*
>
> *Results*
> The subjects who had heard the (b) sentence were likely to say that they had also heard the new sentence (d) since this fitted in with an inference they might reasonably have made. In contrast, subjects who had heard sentence (a) were less likely to think they had heard sentence (c).

Bransford *et al.* cite these findings as showing that people make inferences based on general knowledge; in this case knowledge of spatial relationships between objects like turtles and logs.

SAQ 5
Read the two following short 'stories':
(a) *John was trying to fix the bird house and was pounding the nail when his father came out to watch him.*
(b) *John was trying to fix the bird house and was looking for the nail when his father came out to watch him.*
After hearing which of these sentences do you think it is more likely that people would think that they might have heard: *John was trying to fix the bird house and was using a hammer when his father came out to watch him?*

3.4   The effort after meaning

The significance of all these experiments is that they show that people are not passive receivers of linguistic inputs. As soon as they hear or read the first words in a sentence, they start making inferences about what is likely to come next, taking into account what they have already heard as well as general knowledge about speakers' intentions and the likely topic of discourse.

What happens when people are faced with texts for which they can find no easy interpretation? In circumstances like these, readers will try one interpretation after another, using whatever cues they can. For instance, if I read *I walked into the garden. The chandeliers sparkled brightly*, I might think of light shining through French windows, or possibly of fairy lights. Sentences like *I walked into the sea. The chandeliers were shining brightly* would cause more of a problem. Bransford and his colleagues have carried out some ingenious studies (described in Bransford and McCarrell, 1977) to see how people cope with incomprehensible stories (for an example, see Techniques Box C).

TECHNIQUES BOX C

Bransford and Johnson's Experiment (1972)

Rationale
The authors argue that people are more likely to be able to comprehend and remember a passage of text if they know what it is about. If the appropriate knowledge is not available, people will not be able to make sense of what they hear and will therefore remember very little of it.

Method
Subjects listened to the following passage:

> The procedure is actually quite simple. First you arrange things into different groups. Of course one pile may be sufficient depending on how much there is to do. If you have to go somewhere else due to lack of facilities that is the next step, otherwise you are pretty well set. It is important not to overdo things. That is, it is better to do too few things at once than too many. In the short run this may not seem important but complications can easily arise. A mistake can be expensive as well. At first the whole procedure will seem complicated. Soon, however, it will become just another facet of life. It is difficult to foresee any end to the necessity for this task in the immediate future, but then one never can tell. After the procedure is completed one arranges the materials into different groups again. Then they can be put into their appropriate places. Eventually they will be used once more and the whole cycle will then have to be repeated. However, that is a part of life.

To try this for yourselves, put your hand over the passage and see how much you can remember about it. Now read the passage again but with the additional information that the topic is 'Washing Clothes'.

In Bransford and Johnson's experiment the passage was read out to subjects either with no title, or the title 'Washing Clothes' was presented before hearing the text, or the title was presented after hearing the text but before recall. Subjects were asked to recall the text; this technique of testing *memory for prose* is very commonly used in experiments of this kind. Subjects were also asked to rate the text for comprehensibility.

31

Results
Mean comprehension ratings and recall scores

	No title	Title before	Title after
Comprehension ratings	2.29	4.50	2.12
Recall scores	2.82	5.83	2.65

Comprehension and recall scores were much better for the group who had been given the title before hearing the passage. Note that giving subjects the title after they had already heard the passage did not help them to recall the text.

The knowledge that the topic of the passage is washing clothes enables the listener to make inferences which 'make sense' of the bits about 'going somewhere else if there is a lack of facilities' and the 'arrangement of materials into different piles', and so on. Of course, you will realize that the experimenters chose the passage very cleverly so as to give no clues which would give away what it was about. In fact, you could say that they deliberately broke the 'given-new contract' by not providing any cues about the 'given' topic. Did you nevertheless try to impose some interpretation when you first read the text?

Another technique used by Bransford and Johnson (1973) was to read out an ambiguous passage, giving different groups of subjects different titles. An example is the following text:

Watching a peace march from the fortieth floor
The view was breathtaking. From the window one could see the crowd below. Everything looked extremely small from such a distance, but the colourful costumes could still be seen. Everyone seemed to be moving in one direction in an orderly fashion and there seemed to be little children as well as adults. The landing was gentle and luckily the atmosphere was such that no special suits had to be worn. At first there was a great deal of activity. Later, when the speeches started, the crowd quieted down. The man with the television camera took many shots of the setting and the crowd. Everyone was very friendly and seemed to be glad when the music started.

Put your hand over the passage and try to fill in the missing words in the following sentence:

The landing _____ and luckily the atmosphere _____

Another group of subjects were given the title *A space trip to an inhabited planet.* Read the passage again. Do you feel that the critical sentence would now be easier to remember?

The examples given in this Section demonstrate how people exploit their general knowledge of topics and events in order to generate inferences which enable them to make sense of utterances and texts. In the next Section we shall be discussing how general knowledge is represented in memory. What kinds of mental representations underly people's ability to make inferences about what they hear and read?

Summary of Section 3

- The successful use of language for communication depends on the principle of audience design, which states that utterances are designed to be understood by a particular audience. According to the design assumption, listeners operate on the assumption that speakers expect them to have sufficient shared knowledge to understand an utterance.
- As a result, listeners are constantly making bridging inferences to interpret the meanings of utterances. These include inferences about the reference of given information (given-new contract), inferences about spatial relations (e.g. the turtles example), and causal inferences (e.g. that knives can be murder weapons).
- When subjects make plausible inferences about texts, they are likely to confuse the original wording of sentences with other sentences which express probable inferences.
- Even when a text seems obscure, people try to discover a reasonable interpretation, although they are handicapped in the absence of information about an appropriate topic (i.e. when the given-new contract is broken).

4   Schemas, frames and scripts

The studies described in the previous section certainly demonstrate the importance of general knowledge in language understanding. The next question to consider is how the knowledge stored in each of our memories is organized so that it is always on tap when needed to understand conversations and written texts. Of course, it sometimes seems as if our memories are not at all well-organized.

Bits of knowledge come popping into our minds at odd moments; or fail to come to mind – witness the desperate searching which goes on when we are stumped to remember a name we know perfectly well.

SAQ 6
Answer the following questions:
(a) What is the capital of France?
(b) An anota is a newly discovered bird. Is it likely to have feathers?
(c) If one man mows a meadow in two hours, how long will two men take?

Perhaps our memories are stored in a more organized way than we might think. Otherwise, how were you able to produce the right bits of knowledge to answer the questions in SAQ 6? Although I may not have thought about chandeliers for years, the relevant knowledge was ready to hand when I read Clark's sentence. I didn't know that an 'anota' is a bird – in fact, it certainly isn't one, since I have just made up the name! Yet, if I saw the sentence, *The beautiful and rare anota shook its feathers and took flight,* I'd be convinced that I had understood the sentence correctly as referring to some unknown bird.

One basic problem is that there is no difference between the way we use general knowledge to understand and act in the world about us and the way we use it to understand linguistic inputs. If I see a bird flying across the sky I infer it has feathers. If I am told that the word *anota* is the name of a bird I draw the same inference. The advantage of language is that we can be 'told' so many things, about concepts and events, without having to experience everything for ourselves. Our memories are stuffed full of things we have experienced and things we have been told.

4.1   Schema theory

One theory of memory which has had a great deal of influence on theories of language is schema theory. The basic idea, originally suggested by Bartlett (1932), is that human memory consists of high level structures known as *schemas*, each of which encapsulates our knowledge about everything connected with a particular object or event. This notion has been taken up and expanded to cover many different situations. Examples are schemas for actions, like riding a bicycle, schemas for events, like going to a restaurant, schemas for situations, like working in an office, schemas for categories like birds or mammals.

The organization of memories as schemas guides the interpretation of events, utterances and written texts. For instance, my schema for a room includes information about chandeliers, my schema for a party allows for people leaving for various reasons, my picnic schema helps to make sense of remarks about warm beer.

In the Bransford and Johnson experiment described in Techniques Box C we can think of 'washing clothes' as a schema which made sense of the text. In the 'turtles' experiment in Techniques Box B subjects must have been using a schema about spatial relationships, from which they could infer that some things (turtles) are on top of other things (logs) which are on top of other things (fish). Obviously, too, I have schemas about the exchange of wedding rings, telephone calls, and now I have added the rare 'anota' to my bird schema.

In fact, it is probably fair to say that one of the main problems with schema theory is that it can be used to explain anything. If we remember or use any type of knowledge, we can think up a schema to explain it – perhaps we have a schema for inventing schemas. The trouble with such a flexible notion is that it simply restates the problem of how knowledge is represented, leaving us with the unresolved difficulty of defining how particular schemas are represented and accessed when needed. For this reason, there have been attempts to narrow down the schema concept in specific ways.

You may well be wondering at this point what schema-type representations have to do with understanding language. The point about them is that they represent the general knowledge which aids the understanding of conversations and texts, as well as of real-life events.

4.2   Schemas and frames

Marvin Minsky (1977) wrote a very influential article proposing knowledge schemas for representing different kinds of situations. Minsky called these knowledge representations *frames* because he thought of them as frame-like networks for describing categories of objects and events. You will find when reading articles in psychology journals that the terms schemas and frames are often used more or less interchangeably.

Schemas can be represented as frames which have *slots* which can be filled in with appropriate *values*. Some of these slots have compulsory values; other slots are *variables* which can be filled in with optional values to represent particular situations. Figure 1.1 shows a simple frame to represent some aspects of the schema for representing the concept 'dog'.

DOG

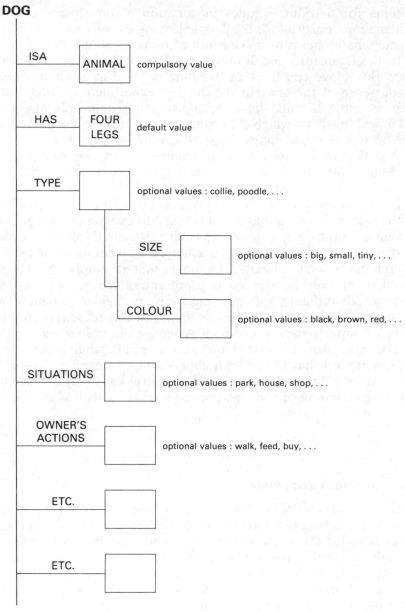

Figure 1.1   A 'dog' frame

You will notice that the slots (shown as boxes in Figure 1.1) cover a wide range of information. For instance, dogs are always animals and usually have four legs, so these slots are filled in with the expected values. Variable slots can be filled in by many different optional values, each of which represents a particular event. If you encounter, or read about, a brown collie in a park, you can fill in the appropriate slots to interpret that particular situation. At the same time the schema will allow you to make inferences about the situation, e.g. is there an owner walking the dog? You will notice that many of the slots are interconnected: a poodle is likely to be small and black and you are more likely to feed a dog in a house than in a shop. Many of the slots invoke other schemas with frames of their own, such as events which are likely to occur in parks, or in shops, e.g. money changes hands. All this helps to make sense of situations and stories in terms of inferences based on probable events.

Many of the inferences described in Section 3 can be thought of as making inferences about probable slot values: for example, that rooms may contain chandeliers or that knives can be used to kill. A particularly useful aspect of frames is that, when specific information is lacking about slots, we can fill them in with what Minsky called *default values*. The idea is that, if nothing else is indicated, by default we select the most commonly expected value for a slot. If I say I am thinking of buying a dog, you would probably make the inference that I have in mind a medium-sized, non-dangerous, four-legged dog. Speakers and writers can take default values for granted, only needing to specify exceptions in special circumstances, e.g. *I've always wanted a three-legged dog!*

SAQ 7
Mary heard the ice-cream truck coming down the street. She remembered her birthday money and rushed into the house. Her daughters wanted some too.
    What strikes you as odd about this story? What default value about Mary's age had you inferred by the end of the second sentence?

A lot of inferences described in previous sections can be explained in terms of assuming default values. When someone is pounding a nail, the default value for the tool he or she is using is a hammer. When you are told that turtles are resting on a floating log, beneath which a fish swam, your default value for the situation is a river or pool. When you are reading about washing clothes, your default value for 'lack of facilities' is not owning a washing-machine.

The range of inferences based on schemas is potentially unlimited. The question is how language users know which schemas are relevant to understanding any particular text. In Section 4.3 I shall be describing an attempt to show how knowledge of probable events can be used to generate inferences about the meanings of stories.

4.3   Scripts

Minsky used the special term *scenario* for frames which describe events. This idea has been extended by Roger Schank and his colleagues (e.g. Schank and Abelson, 1977a, 1977b) in the form of *scripts*, which describe simple routine events. A 'Restaurant' script is shown in Figure 1.2.

Name: Restaurant

Props:	Tables	*Roles*:	Customer
	Menu		Waiter/waitress
	Food		Cook
	Bill		Cashier
	Money		Owner
	Tip		

Entry conditions: Customer is hungry   *Results*: Customer has less money
                    Customer has money   Owner has more money
                                                    Customer is not hungry

---

Scene 1: Entering
          Customer enters restaurant
          Customer looks for table
          Customer decides where to sit
          Customer goes to table
          Customer sits down

Scene 2: Ordering
          Waitress brings menu
          Customer reads menu
          Customer decides on food
          Customer orders food
          Waitress gives food order to cook
          Cook prepares food

Scene 3: Eating
          Cook gives food to waitress
          Waitress brings food to customer
          Customer eats food

Scene 4: Exiting
          Customer asks for bill
          Waitress gives bill to customer
          Customer gives tip to waitress
          Customer goes to cashier
          Customer gives money to cashier
          Customer leaves restaurant

Figure 1.2 Restaurant script (adapted from Bower, Black and Turner, 1979)

Perhaps the best way to think about scripts is that they list the default values for actions which you would expect to occur in any restaurant. Actual events on a particular visit to a particular restaurant can be represented by filling in the slots for 'roles', 'props' and 'actions'. The sentence *When John Brown went to McDonalds he recognized one of the waitresses* would be interpreted by allocating McDonalds to the restaurant name slot, John Brown to the customer role and a friend to the waitress role. In the absence of any other information, it would be inferred from the default values that John looked at the menu, ordered, paid, and ended up less hungry but poorer than when entering the restaurant.

SAQ 8
John went to a fast-food restaurant and ordered a hamburger. He thought it was disgusting and left a very small tip.
(a) List the slots in the Restaurant script which need to be filled in to understand this 'story'.
(b) What inferences have to be made to explain John's behaviour?

The notion of scripts is important for theories of language because Schank and his colleagues incorporated scripts into a computer program for understanding stories about events like visiting restaurants. Script information about roles and events was typed into the computer. Subsequently short 'stories' were typed in and the computer used the information in the scripts to produce an interpretation based on inferences about the normal order of events in restaurants. The program was called *SAM*, standing for *Script Applier Mechanism*. A sample of SAM's input and output is shown in Figure 1.3 overleaf; SAM's output is shown in capital letters.

Despite the impressive performance of SAM in understanding simple stories about restaurants, Schank has himself pointed out some of the inadequacies of scripts as a complete explanation of the role of inferences in language understanding. For one thing, there would have to be an enormous proliferation of scripts for all possible sequences of events: dressing in the morning, catching a bus, going on an aeroplane, buying things in a supermarket, going to the hairdresser, going to the doctor, going to the dentist, and so on, and so on.

Schank is one of the few researchers trying to develop computer programs who is also interested in the findings of psychology experiments. Some interesting experiments to see whether humans use scripts when comprehending and remembering stories are described in Techniques Box D.

Input:
John went to a restaurant. The waiter gave John a menu. The waiter came to the table. John ordered lobster. John was served quickly. John left a large tip.

Questions and answers:
Q: What did John eat?
A: LOBSTER
Q: Who gave John the menu?
A: THE WAITER
Q: Who gave John the lobster?
A: PROBABLY THE WAITER
Q: Who paid the bill?
A: PROBABLY JOHN
Q: What happened when John went to the table?
A: JOHN SAT DOWN AND THE WAITER GAVE HIM A MENU
Q: Why did John get a menu?
A: SO HE COULD ORDER
Q: Why did John give the waiter a large tip?
A: BECAUSE HE WAS SERVED QUICKLY

Paraphrase:
JOHN WENT TO A RESTAURANT. JOHN LOOKED FOR A TABLE. JOHN WENT TO THE TABLE. JOHN SAT DOWN IN THE CHAIR. JOHN GOT THE MENU FROM THE WAITER. JOHN READ THE MENU. THE WAITER WENT TO THE TABLE. JOHN ORDERED LOBSTER. THE COOK PREPARED THE LOBSTER. THE WAITER GOT THE LOBSTER FROM THE COOK. THE WAITER SERVED JOHN THE LOBSTER. JOHN ATE THE LOBSTER. JOHN INDICATED TO THE WAITER HE WOULD LIKE TO GET THE BILL FROM HIM. JOHN GOT THE BILL FROM THE WAITER. JOHN LEFT THE WAITER A LARGE TIP. JOHN PAID THE BILL. JOHN LEFT THE RESTAURANT

Summary:
JOHN WENT TO A RESTAURANT AND ATE LOBSTER

Figure 1.3   Dialogue with SAM (adapted from Schank and Abelson, 1977a)

SAQ 9
List some inferences in the paraphrase which are not stated in the input story.

TECHNIQUES BOX D

Bower, Black and Turner's Experiments (1979)

Rationale
The idea behind these experiments was to test whether people would agree about which events occur in particular scripts; and also to see whether scripts would affect the way subjects remember stories based on script situations.

Method
Bower *et al.* first asked their subjects to write a list of actions people would normally perform in certain situations, like going to a restaurant, attending a lecture, and visiting a doctor. In a second

---

experiment subjects read story texts, which described different versions of script-based activities, like going to a restaurant or visiting a doctor. *Ss* read either 1, 2 or 3 versions of each script story, e.g. Visiting the doctor and Visiting the dentist are two versions of the Visiting health professional script. They were later asked to write down what they could recall of each story. The prediction was that subjects would falsely 'remember' some probable script actions even though they did not occur in the original stories.

Results
When the lists of actions produced by subjects for each script situation were compared, a great deal of agreement was found about the main events, as shown in Figure 1.4. For instance, attending a lecture involves entering a room, finding a seat, taking out a notebook, taking notes, checking the time, and – possibly with a feeling of relief – leaving at the end.

In the second experiment, subjects' recalls for script stories were scored according to whether the remembered actions had been mentioned in the texts (stated actions) or could be inferred from the

Attending a lecture
ENTER ROOM
Look for friends
FIND SEAT
SIT DOWN
Settle belongings
TAKE OUT NOTEBOOK
Look at other students
Talk
Look at professor
LISTEN TO PROFESSOR
TAKE NOTES
CHECK TIME
Ask questions
Change position in seat
Daydream
Look at other students
Take more notes
Close notebook
Gather belongings
Stand up
Talk
LEAVE

Visiting a doctor
Enter office
CHECK IN WITH RECEPTIONIST
SIT DOWN
Wait
Look at other people
READ MAGAZINE
Name called
Follow nurse
Enter examination room
Undress
Sit on table
Talk to nurse
NURSE TESTS
Wait
Doctor enters
Doctor greets
Talk to doctor about problem
Doctor asks questions
DOCTOR EXAMINES
Get dressed
Get medicine
Make another appointment
LEAVE OFFICE

Note: Events in capital letters were mentioned by most subjects, items in italics by fewer subjects, and items in ordinary print by fewest subjects.

Figure 1.4 Agreed script actions (adapted from Bower, Black and Turner, 1979)

script but were not actually mentioned in the text (unstated actions). As shown in the table, although more stated script actions were remembered, subjects also 'recalled' a considerable number of unstated inferred script actions as well.

Number of script versions	Recall of stated script actions	Recall of unstated script actions	Recall of other actions
1	3.03	0.80	0.39
2	2.27	1.26	0.35
3	2.56	1.16	0.36

As you can see in the table, this effect was more marked for people who had read two or three versions of each type of script, presumably because they began to muddle up which of the stated actions had occurred in which story. Recall of unstated actions included cases when people thought they had read *John arrived at the doctor's office*, which had been unstated in the 'doctor' story, because a similar sentence *Bill arrived at the dentist's office* had been stated in the 'dentist' story.

SAQ 10
Write down some actions which you think should be included in a Getting up in the morning script.

The results of Bower *et al.*'s experiment have been interpreted as showing that not all scripts are at the level of particular sequences of events. People may have specific scripts for visiting doctors or dentists. But they also have more general superordinate scripts which contain the events common to all visits to professionals. It is these more general scripts which lead to confusions between actions which are equally likely to occur in the waiting rooms of doctors, dentists, chiropodists and lawyers.

This proposal appears to cut down the need for an enormous proliferation of individual scripts for each type of event. Actions which are common to many events can be incorporated into general scripts, e.g. visiting all types of offices, attending all kinds of performances, paying for all services. But this in turn raises the problem of how people know which level of information is necessary for understanding a particular story.

Schank shows that even a simple utterance like *My drain pipe is overflowing* may require many different kinds of information, going far beyond a Plumber script, in order to understand possible responses like *I know a good plumber; Boy that's going to cost you a lot of money; I told you not to get such an old house; And with your mother coming to visit.* The problem of which schemas need to be activated to aid understanding of particular utterances remains an extremely difficult issue for cognitive psychology.

4.4   Goals and plans

Many researchers into language understanding have suggested that it is impossible to understand stories without taking into account the goals, plans and intentions of the participants. The kinds of 'stories' input to SAM about restaurants are very dull. The example given in Figure 1.3 is not really a story at all; nor could you imagine two sane people having a conversation about John's behaviour without asking why he chose lobster or decided to leave a large tip.

On the other hand, as Schank (1982a) points out, we find little difficulty in understanding sentences like *John wanted to become king. He went to get some arsenic.* It is most improbable that there is a special script for 'killing kings' which involves a series of actions which includes buying arsenic. It is because we understand John's ultimate goal that we are able to interpret his interest in arsenic as part of a plan.

Suppose the story had been *John wanted to be king. He went to the chemist shop.* We would still try to interpret the second sentence as part of a plan. Using our knowledge of the Shopping script, we might infer that John is filling the customer role, that some kind of poison is being bought, and that money will be exchanged.

SAQ 11
(a) *John felt hungry. He went to fetch a sandwich.*
(b) *John felt hungry. He went to fetch the Good Food Guide.*
Which of these two stories requires more 'bridging' inferences in order to understand the connection between John's goal and his plan to achieve that goal?

Lehnert (1981) attempted to formalize stories in terms of people's goals and actions. Figure 1.5 shows a list of some *primitive plot units* from which stories can be built up. The idea is that these plot units can be combined to make up more complex plot units which involve sequences of goals, plans and outcomes. For instance, a story could be interpreted as an example of 'starting over' if it includes the sequence of plot units: success – loss – problem – perseverance.

PROBLEM

You get fired and need a job.
You bounce a check and need to deposit funds.
Your dog dies and you long for companionship.

SUCCESS

You ask for a raise and you get it.
You fix a flat tire.
You need a car so you steal one.

FAILURE

Your proposal of marriage is declined.
You can't find your wallet.
You can't get a bank loan.

RESOLUTION

Your broken radio starts working again.
They catch the thief who has your wallet.
You fix a flat tire after a blow out.

LOSS

Your big income tax refund is a mistake.
The woman you love leaves you.
The car you just bought is totaled.

PERSEVERANCE

You want to get married (again).
You reapply to Yale after being rejected.
You want to ski again after a bad skiing accident.

HIDDEN BLESSING

You get audited and they owe you.
You sprain an ankle and win damages.
Your mother dies and you inherit a million.

MIXED BLESSING

You buy a car and it turns out to be a lemon.
You fall in love and become insanely jealous.
Your book is reviewed but they hate it.

Figure 1.5   Examples of primitive plot units (adapted from Lehnert, 1981)

SAQ 12
Allocate the following events to one of the primitive plot units listed in Figure 1.5.
(a) *Your car breaks down.*
(b) *You pass an exam.*
(c) *You buy a dog that costs a lot to feed.*
(d) *You reapply to the Open University next year.*

One point you should notice about the use of goals and plans to understand stories is that they are based on people's motives and intentions in real-life situations. In fact, all the schemas we have discussed so far have been based on experiences of the world, including being told things. Clark's bridging inferences depend on general knowledge about rooms and chandeliers, about dislike of warm beer – at least in America; Bransford *et al.*'s experiments rely on people knowing that turtles, logs and fish can all exist in water, and about likely occurrences on peace marches and space-ship landings; Schank's scripts encapsulate what we know about eating in restaurants and going to the doctor.

According to this view, the schemas necessary for understanding language are identical with the schemas used for understanding the world about us and the motives behind people's actions. People use language to communicate about things which are important to them. Instead of reaching over to grab the salt, I am likely to say *Please pass the salt.* Instead of going ahead and digging up the whole garden, it is more cost-effective to have a discussion about where to plant the dahlias this year. Instead of constantly asking *What do you mean?* and *Who are you talking about?*, life is likely to be pleasanter if listeners try to make inferences based on general knowledge about what speakers are likely to be referring to and what meanings they are trying to convey.

It seems likely though, in addition to general knowledge about what happens in real-life situations, people also have schemas which represent their expectations about the form of linguistic inputs, especially stories and texts.

4.5   *Story schemas and story grammars*

The basic notion of *story schemas* is that we know something about how all stories are structured, over and above the content of any particular story. The only way we can know this is from experiences of hearing and reading many stories, all of which conform to a typical structure.

When you think of all the different kinds of stories you may have read – novels, collections of short stories, children's stories, newspaper stories – you may well wonder if there are any rules which can define a single typical structure for all stories. Several psychologists have proposed that, at least for fiction, all the different 'surface' forms of stories can be interpreted in terms of a 'deep' underlying structure which is universal to all stories. This deep structure can be defined by a sct of rules known as a *story grammar*.

The rules in a story grammar are of a special type known as *rewrite rules*. This means that the structure of a story can be defined in terms of rules which can be used to 'rewrite' the story into its component parts. Figure 1.6 shows a set of grammar rules for simple stories proposed by Thorndyke (1977).

What these rules mean is that, according to Rule 1, a STORY can first be broken down into a SETTING followed by a THEME followed by a PLOT followed by a RESOLUTION. Rule 2 states that the SETTING can be rewritten as consisting of information about CHARACTERS, the LOCATION and TIME at which the

Rule number	Rule
1	STORY $\longrightarrow$ SETTING + THEME + PLOT + RESOLUTION
2	SETTING $\longrightarrow$ CHARACTERS + LOCATION + TIME
3	THEME $\longrightarrow$ GOAL
4	PLOT $\longrightarrow$ EPISODE(S)
5	EPISODE $\longrightarrow$ SUBGOAL + ATTEMPT(S) + OUTCOME
6	ATTEMPT $\longrightarrow$ EVENT(S)
7	RESOLUTION $\longrightarrow$ EVENT and/or STATE
8	GOAL $\longrightarrow$ DESIRED STATE

Figure 1.6 Grammar rules for simple stories (adapted from Thorndyke, 1977)

story takes place. According to Rule 3 the THEME can be rewritten as stating the GOAL of the main character. Rule 4 states that the PLOT consists of one or more EPISODES, which themselves include SUBGOALS, ATTEMPTS (involving EVENTS), and OUTCOMES (Rules 5–6). Finally, Rules 7 and 8 state that the RESOLUTION consists of an EVENT or a STATE which is a DESIRED STATE in terms of the original GOAL as stated in the THEME.

Let us take a simple story as an example (each phrase in the story is identified by a number):

Once upon a time (1) a prince and princess (2) were walking in the forest (3). The prince wanted to marry the princess (4). He asked her to marry him (5). She said yes (6). They got married and lived happily ever after (7).

Figure 1.7 shows how story grammar rules can be used to generate a structure for this particular story. Structures of this kind are known as *tree structures* because they consist of *nodes* which branch out from a single node, the STORY. (You will notice that it is really an upside-down tree with the trunk at the top and the branches at the bottom.) One characteristic of rewrite rules is that you go on rewriting the nodes until you get down to the actual phrases in the story (known as *terminal nodes* because they are filled in at the bottom of the tree structure with actual story events).

Apart from being an exceedingly simple story, this analysis shows that goals and subgoals are often not explicitly stated in a story but have to be inferred from the actions of the characters. The claim is

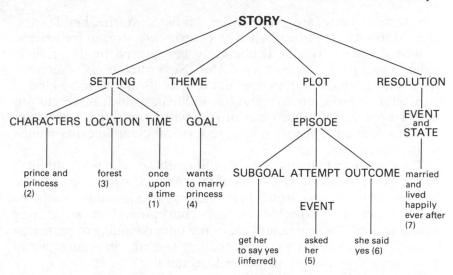

Figure 1.7 Tree structure for a simple story

that, while the rules may allow certain 'surface' elements to be omitted, we cannot understand the 'deep' structure of a story unless we infer the missing goals and subgoals.

It has been shown (Thorndyke, 1977) that leaving out crucial elements like the THEME or altering the order of story components makes stories harder to understand and remember. In general, the more a story conforms to the 'ideal' structure set out by the grammar, the easier it is to understand. Stories with an ideal structure are said to reflect a *canonical* story format. On the other hand, stories with such predictable structures tend to be rather boring – at least for adult readers.

Mandler and Johnson (1977) make the point that story grammars are particularly suitable for folk-tales which are passed on orally from generation to generation before being written down. The reason why traditional story-tellers are able to recite long complex stories from memory is that the stories conform to an underlying structure in which a single protagonist carries out a series of actions to achieve a stated goal. Regardless of how many events occur in the story, a teller can keep track of the overall framework of the story. It has often been noted that story-tellers produce slightly different versions of a basic story on each occasion, showing that they have memorized, not a word-perfect surface version, but rather the underlying deep structure which enables them to generate the events in the story.

Naturally, there are many other kinds of stories besides traditional folk-tales. Particularly when stories are written for reading at leisure, elements may deliberately be omitted or distorted in order to surprise, as in mystery stories. Nevertheless, as readers we often feel cheated if a story does not resolve itself into some kind of satisfactory conclusion. We also have schemas which represent our expectations about other types of text with very different conventions: for instance, history books, reports of scientific experiments, airline timetables.

The story grammarians (e.g. Mandler, 1982) claim that, although people are normally unconscious of the rules for structuring stories, they nevertheless have stored in memory some kind of story schema which represents expected literary conventions for structuring typical stories. These schemas aid in the understanding of particular stories by enabling listeners and readers to make inferences about the underlying structure of stories in general.

Black and Wilensky (1979) have argued that there is no need to postulate special story schemas. All that is necessary is an understanding of people's goals and motivations in real-life situations. Since stories are about people, they will naturally describe people's usual behaviour. If you look back to the primitive plot units listed in Figure 1.5, you will see that the prince and princess story could also be analysed as a combination of primitive plot units representing motivations and actions:

PROBLEM *Prince wants to marry princess.*

SUCCESS *When prince asks princess she says yes.*

RESOLUTION *They marry and live happily ever after.*

It is certainly not at all easy to disentangle story schemas from our general knowledge about goals and actions. Some cognitive psychologists (e.g. Van Dijk and Kintsch, 1983) accept the compromise position that there are indeed literary conventions governing stories and other kinds of texts irrespective of content. We do expect stories to have a beginning, a middle and an end and to deal with interesting, funny or unexpected characters and situations. On the other hand, our knowledge of characters' goals and plans is based on experiences of the world about us, even when the action is transplanted to a far-flung planet, as in a science-fiction story.

Summary of Section 4

- One of the biggest issues for theories of language understanding is how to represent general knowledge as it is used in making inferences about utterances and texts.
- Bartlett's notion of schemas for organizing memory representations of objects, situations and events has been reformulated by Minsky (1977) as frames. These are networks with slots which can be filled in with compulsory or optional values. In the absence of information about a particular situation, default values represent general expectations.
- Schank developed Minsky's notion of scenario frames into scripts which represent sequences of routine actions, like the Restaurant script.
- Knowledge of people's goals and plans is necessary in order to understand stories about human actions.
- Story grammars define rules for formulating the underlying structures of typical stories; these rules are internalized as story schemas.

5   Some conclusions

Perhaps you are still wondering what schemas, frames, scripts, story grammars and story schemas have to do with language and communication. The point I have been trying to get across is that communication depends on speakers' and listeners' knowledge. If they share a lot of knowledge, communication is easy. Between husband and wife, close friends or colleagues, it may be enough to say 'his usual self' or even just to raise your eyes in exasperation. In more formal conversations, it may be necessary to indicate precisely the information which will activate an appropriate frame or script. Both speaker and listener have to be aware of the kinds of inferences that are likely to be made on the basis of knowledge about objects, events and speaker intentions (the audience design assumption).

According to schema theory, all these types of knowledge consist of schemas which organize our memories for typical events, situations and literary conventions. Scripts, goals and story grammars can all be thought of as frames with terminal slots, which are filled in to represent particular inputs. When we read about a visit to a restaurant or hear a folk-tale, we map what we see or hear on to the frame which represents expectations about that event. If any information is missing, we infer what the speaker or writer must have meant from our knowledge of commonly accepted default values.

Although schemas for representing scripts, goals and stories have been described separately, there is no doubt that all these sources of knowledge are used simultaneously in language understanding. We use general knowledge schemas to make bridging inferences about what utterances and texts are referring to; we use story schemas to infer themes and plots; we use schema representations of goals and plans to interpret speakers' intentions.

One important point to note about the approach discussed so far is that it has taken for granted people's ability to understand the literal meanings of sentences, i.e. that the squiggles on this page can be identified as English words and that these words make up grammatical sentences. It is only if we can identify the words *prince* and *princess* and understand the significance of the phrase *wants to marry* that we can begin to interpret this sequence of words as a reasonable goal for a prince in a fairy tale.

There is no point in discussing how language users interpret stories about restaurants, make inferences about whether turtles are resting, appreciate the significance of sentences about warm beer, if they can't read or understand English in the first place. General knowledge is needed for interpreting communications, but something else must be involved in being able to speak, read and understand English or any other language.

The distinction I am drawing is between general knowledge about the world, on the one hand, as opposed to specifically linguistic knowledge, on the other. Part I has been concerned with general knowledge. Parts II and III will consider the no less complex topic of how linguistic knowledge is represented in memory and how it is used to process linguistic inputs.

Further reading

Schank has written an interesting little book, *Reading and Understanding* (1982a), in which he presents his theories about scripts in the form of guidance to teachers of reading. The book also introduces other aspects of Schank's theory which will be discussed in Parts II and III.

Thinking: Readings in Cognitive Science (1977), edited by Johnson-Laird and Wason, includes several important articles quoted in the text: an article on frames by Minsky; an account of the experiments by Bransford and McCarrell; the 'bridging' article by Clark; and an introduction to scripts by Schank and Abelson.

Part II
Representations and Processes

Judith Greene

Part II   Representations and Processes

Contents

1   Introduction

Part I introduced the notion that people cannot understand language without knowing something about the context in which an utterance occurs. They use general knowledge about the world to make inferences about what meanings a speaker or writer is intending to convey. This involves a lot of high level knowledge about the world (schemas), events which are likely to occur (scripts) and social conventions for different types of communication (story schemas and speech acts). Participants in a conversation, or readers of a text, are constantly drawing inferences about what a particular linguistic input means. If we know nothing about a topic, we won't be able to make the 'bridging' inferences necessary to understand sentences which assume that knowledge.

On the other hand, as I pointed out at the end of Part I, language speakers and understanders also have to know the sounds, written letters, words and grammar of a language in order to communicate effectively. If everything about language and understanding could be explained as being due to general knowledge, why do we find it so difficult to make our intentions understood in a language we don't know? Even if I appreciate the social context and probable intentions of, say, a Hungarian speaker, I find it impossible to carry on a meaningful conversation unless we happen to share knowledge of a common language. Equally, I cannot understand a text in all the many languages I don't know how to read, including Shivasi!

In terms of the types of knowledge discussed in Section 2 of Part I, language users need to know the lexical meanings of individual words, grammatical rules (syntax), semantic rules for interpreting sentences, discourse rules for interpreting texts and pragmatic rules for interpreting speech acts as indicators of speakers' intentions. Before going on to discuss theories about how all these types of linguistic knowledge are represented in memory, it is important to draw your attention to two distinctions.

The first has already been mentioned in the introduction to Part I: the dichotomy between *competence* and *performance*. One of the most influential modern theories of language is Noam Chomsky's theory of transformational grammar. Chomsky is a linguist who is concerned with specifying linguistic rules which define the ideal competence of a language speaker. It is psychologists who try to translate these linguistic rules into models which explain the actual performance of language users when they produce and understand particular utterances. The tension between purely linguistic competence and the many other factors which affect language performance will be one of the major themes of Part II.

The second contrast is between language representations and language processes. It has been common practice in psychological theories to distinguish between *knowledge representations*, the *processes* which operate on the basis of that knowledge and representations of *linguistic inputs*. You will find that many of the theories discussed in later sections assume some kind of distinction between representations of permanent knowledge in long-term memory, the processing of linguistic inputs, and the resulting representations of sentence meanings.

This approach to language is often formulated as an *information processing model*. As shown in Figure 2.1, there is a strong implication that information is processed in a series of stages. Notice that this is a *linear model* in the sense that information flows in a left to right direction, implying *bottom-up processing* of linguistic inputs through the various stages to the top level of discourse processing. Nevertheless, at all processing stages, knowledge of linguistic rules stored in memory is deployed in *top-down processing* of the input, as shown in the 'memory cloud' in Figure 2.1. Thus, the model in Figure 2.1 allows for *interactive processing* between two sources of knowledge: inputs from the outside world and information already stored in memory.

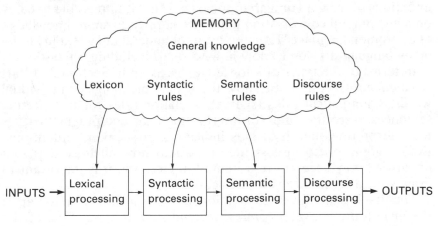

Figure 2.1   Linear stage model of language processing

On the other hand, the information processing model assumes separate stages for the various types of processing, implying that each stage of processing has to be completed before the next stage can begin. A stage model of this kind is called a *hierarchical model* because there is a hierarchy of separate processing levels. According to Figure 2.1, syntactic processing has to produce a complete analysis of sentences before semantic processing can begin. As we shall see, there has been a lot of controversy about whether processing stages can be separated in this way.

By now you should be aware that explaining how we are able to understand language is not an easy matter. In the next sections I shall be addressing four major questions:

1 How are the meanings of individual words represented in the lexicon?
2 What role do syntactic rules play in language processing?
3 How are the meanings of sentences processed and represented?
4 What principles of discourse processing are involved in the interpretation of texts?

Summary of Section 1

- Linguistic knowledge has traditionally been defined as including a lexicon of word meanings, a syntactic component containing syntactic rules, a semantic component containing semantic rules for extracting sentence meanings and a discourse component containing discourse rules, such as story grammars and speech acts, for interpreting texts and conversations.
- Linguistic theories (e.g. Noam Chomsky's theory of transformational grammar) define the linguistic rules which constitute linguistic competence. Psychologists study the role of knowledge representations and linguistic processing in language performance.
- Many theories of language have assumed a linear information processing model in which linguistic inputs are processed by a hierarchical series of processing stages, each of which has to be completed before going on to the next stage.

2   The lexicon

Most theories of language agree that language users must have some sort of *lexicon* stored in memory. When we hear or read words it is assumed that the patterns of sounds or letters are recognized because they correspond to a *lexical item* in our mental lexicons. But what are these lexical items like and how do they represent the meanings of words? It may at first appear as if this is an easy question, but in fact most words have many slightly different meanings.

2.1   Word meanings

The ability to recognize words is not a simple perceptual skill, since words are made up of arbitrary sequences of sounds and letters. For instance, English speakers can recognize and pronounce the word *tree* whereas French speakers can recognize and pronounce *arbre*, the French word for tree. As you will certainly appreciate if you have tried to learn the vocabulary of a foreign language, it is no easy task to learn the connections between words and their meanings. Moreover, word meanings not only determine how words should be used but often affect the way they should be pronounced. The word *bank* is easy enough to pronounce but what about *sow*? Should it rhyme with *low* or *cow*? This clearly depends on which meaning of the three letters *s-o-w* is intended. On the other hand, the word *bank* may have only one pronunciation but has several meanings.

SAQ 13
(a) Write down two sentences, one of which might lead someone to pronounce *bow* to rhyme with *low* and the other to rhyme with *bough*.
(b) Write down at least three meanings for the word *bank*.

The vocabulary problem is highlighted by the fact that in French the word *banque* refers only to a financial institution. The French word for a river bank is *rive* which can also be used to refer to a beach or coastline. Trying to specify all the possible senses of words, as in a dictionary, is a never-ending task. It was only when I was looking up the word for river bank in my French dictionary that I noticed that *rivière de diamants* means a diamond necklace, an enchanting phrase although 'river of diamonds' would have quite a different sense in English. The problem is, if words can have so many different meanings, how do we know which sense is intended? If the word *bank* is so ambiguous, how do we know when it means a financial institution or a river edge?

While some words are relatively easy to define by pointing to an object or a picture, e.g. *camel*, *zebra* or *unicorn*, many – perhaps most – depend on the context in which they occur. There is, for instance, unlikely to be much confusion about *I needed some money so I went to the bank*. A nice demonstration of the importance of context in defining word meanings comes from Schank (1982a). Schank took as an example the way that an apparently simple word like *took* changes its meaning according to the sentence in which it occurs. The primary meaning of *took* might be thought of as implying that one person has taken something away from someone else. But does this cover the meaning of *took* in all the following sentences?

John took the book.

John took an aeroplane.

John took an aspirin.

John took the job.

John took my advice.

Schank took as an example . . .

All these sentences seem to share a common core of meaning and yet there are subtle distinctions, as shown by the fact that the word *grabbed*, which might be thought of as a synonym for *took*, only sounds right in the first sentence. A *synonym* is a word with an identical or similar meaning.

SAQ 14
Write down an appropriate synonym word or phrase for *gave* in each of the following sentences:
(a) *John gave Mary a (wedding) ring.*
(b) *John gave Mary a (telephone) ring.*
(c) *John gave Mary a cold.*
(d) *John gave in.*
(e) *John gave notice.*

The difference between dictionaries and psychological theories of language is that the latter aim to describe how people know which sense of a word to select in any particular context. Why do language understanders find no problem in deciding that *the pen in the box* implies quite a different meaning for the word *pen* as compared with *the box in the pen?* Why are we usually quite unaware of the possible ambiguity of thc word *ring* in a scntcncc rcfcrring to a ring for your finger or a telephone call?

In the next sections, I shall be describing three approaches to tackling the problem of representing word meanings in such a way that the correct senses of words can be selected: semantic features, case frames and semantic primitives.

2.2   Semantic features

The basic idea is that all the words in the lexicon can be defined in terms of sets of *semantic features*. Katz and Fodor (1963) proposed a theory in which words are defined in terms of features like animate, inanimate, human, animal, physical object, activity. Each sense of a word would have to be allocated different features, as shown for the word *ball* in Figure 2.2.

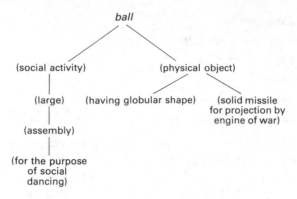

Figure 2.2   Semantic features (adapted from Katz and Fodor, 1963)

Another way of expressing information about semantic features is to list for each sense of a word whether it has a feature (+) or doesn't have it (−). An example would be *ball* (+ physical object) (− human) and *ball* (+ social activity) (+ large) (+ assembly).

SAQ 15
Write down some features (+ and −) for the word *bachelor*.

The main purpose of defining words in this way is to specify rules about which combinations of words make sense. These rules are known as *selection restrictions* because they restrict the selection of word combinations to those which are compatible. For example, the adjective *sincere* cannot be combined with an inanimate object, as in *sincere stone*. Selection restrictions can be formulated by referring to general semantic features which rule out many different nonsensical combinations. A single rule which states that all adjectives which have the feature (+ moral evaluation) are not allowed to be combined with objects with the feature (− human) rules out many combinations like *despairing table, happy needle, conscientious banana.*

SAQ 16
(a) What semantic feature might be needed to define possible subjects of the verb *admire*?
(b) What semantic features might be needed to define possible objects of *admire*?

To see how selection restrictions work, let us take as an example a sentence like *He hit the ball*. The word 'hit' would have a list of features indicating that it has two possible senses:

1 the sense of 'strike' with an instrument, which requires (+ human) as subject and (+ physical object) for its instrument and object, e.g. *The man hit the ball with a bat;* and
2 the sense of 'collide' which can refer to any two physical objects, e.g. *The rock hit the car.*

SAQ 17
Looking at the definitions given above for *hit*, indicate which of the following sentences are acceptable and why:
(a) *Peter hit the rock with a ball.*
(b) *The car hit a truck with a ball.*
(c) *A rock hit Peter.*
(d) *John hit Peter at the ball.*

The acceptability of sentence (d) raises some problems for semantic feature theories. It is not easy to see how the fact that a dance is a place where things like hitting can occur can be incorporated into the semantic features of the individual word 'dance'. The 'dance' sense of ball in Figure 2.2 would need to have features specifying all possible occurrences which could take place at a dance. Another problem with attaching semantic features to individual words is that the same features would have to be repeated for all words with a similar meaning; 'dance', 'ball', 'party', 'rave-up', 'race meeting', 'wedding' would all have to be defined as social activities where things can happen. This would result in very complex feature lists for each word in the lexicon.

2.3   Case frames

Semantic features define word meanings so that selection restriction rules can specify permitted and non-permitted combinations of meanings, e.g. hitting a tennis ball as opposed to hitting a dance. Another quite different approach is to define words directly in terms of the sentence contexts in which they can occur.

One of the most common types of analysis of sentence contexts is known as *case grammar*. First proposed by the linguist Fillmore (1968), the basic idea is to analyse sentences into 'cases' attached to the verb. The main cases are listed below:

Agent: animate being who initiates action

Instrument: inanimate entity which is involved in the action

Recipient: animate being who is affected by the action

Object: inanimate entity which is affected by the action

Locative: the location or direction of the action

The Object is defined as any inanimate entity which is affected by the verb, whether or not it is the grammatical object of the verb. For instance, in *The picture was painted by John*, the *picture* would be the Object because it is affected by being painted by John (the Agent). In a sentence like *The key opened the door*, the *key* is treated as an Instrument (with an unstated Agent) and the *door* as the Object which is affected by 'opening'.

SAQ 18
Indicate the appropriate cases under the nouns in the following sentences:
(a) *John broke the window with a hammer.*
(b) *The hammer broke the window.*
(c) *John invited Mary to a party.*

According to case grammar, the lexicon would define each meaning of a verb in terms of the cases it can take. Thus the 'strike' sense of *hit* would be defined as needing an Agent, an Object and a possible Instrument. The 'collide' sense of *hit* would be defined as taking two Objects because both the objects involved in a collision are affected by the action expressed by the verb. Case frames are often represented as diagrams, as shown in Figure 2.3.

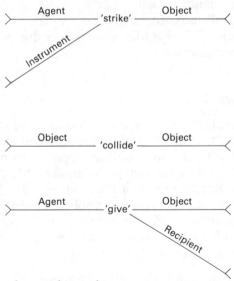

Figure 2.3 Case frames for verbs

The diagrams in Figure 2.3 represent *case frames* for verbs. Represented in this way it is clear that it is no coincidence that these are known as frames. The definitions shown in Figure 2.3 are frames with case slots which specify which kinds of words can be filled in as values. For the verb *strike* the Agent and Object slots have to be filled in but the Instrument slot is optional.

One commonly used representation for case frames is based on *predicate calculus*. The verb is specified as a *predicate* and the cases as *arguments* of that predicate. The predicate verbs and arguments (shown in brackets) for *strike* and *collide* would be:

> *strike* (Agent, Object, Instrument)
>
> *collide* (Object 1, Object 2)

SAQ 19
Express the verb *give* as a predicate and arguments. HINT: Look at the case frame representation for *give* in Figure 2.3.

Whichever notation is used, it is important to stress one difference between case frames and semantic features. Features can go into more semantic detail than cases. The feature selection restrictions for *collide* are defined as requiring objects with the feature (+ physical object). However, the Object case is defined more generally as *any* inanimate entity which is affected by an action. So what is to stop you filling in the slots of *collide* with the inanimate entities *sincerity* and *smoke*, as in *Sincerity collided with smoke*? It is for this reason that psychologists adapted Fillmore's original linguistic formulation of case in order to allow for more semantic restrictions. As we shall see in Section 2.4, they have done this by specifying more precisely what kinds of nouns can go with which kinds of verbs.

The problem of word meanings is not an easy one though. It is simple enough to say that a word like *eat* takes an Agent and an Object which is affected by the action, or that it requires the semantic features (+ animate) for its Subject and (+ physical) for its Object. This certainly prevents completely unacceptable combinations like *He eats sincerity* but presumably does allow *He eats the table*. What is really needed is a selection restriction for the object of *eat* which restricts it to potentially edible objects. However, while *Cows eat meat* may be more acceptable than *Cows eat sincerity*, ideally a semantic theory should be able to specify fine gradations of meaning, e.g. that *cows eat grass*. So *grass* would have the features (+ eatable) (+ cows). *Meat* could be defined as (+ eatable) (+ carnivores). *Honey* would need to have the features (+ eatable) (+ humans) (+ bees), (+ bears); in other words, a list of animate entities which like to eat honey. And, of course, cars only eat petrol!

2.4   Semantic primitives

Rather than attributing features to whole words, some researchers
have attempted to capture the semantic core of word meanings by
'decomposing' their meanings into a small set of *semantic primitives*. Schank (1972) drew up a list of 12–15 *primitive actions* which
he claims underly the meanings of all verbs which describe actions.
Listed below are some of Schank's main primitives, which he calls
Acts:

ATRANS: transfer of possession

PTRANS: physical transfer from one location to another

MTRANS: transfer of mental information

MBUILD: build memory structures

ATTEND: sensory input (seeing, hearing, etc.)

PROPEL: application of force to physical object

MOVE: move a body part

INGEST: intake of food, air

EXPEL: the reverse of ingest!

SAQ 20
List the primitive Acts which best express the meanings of the verbs in the
following sentences:
(a) *Mary gave John a book.*
(b) *Mary gave John some advice.*
(c) *Mary took a plane.*
(d) *Mary took an aspirin.*
(e) *Mary raised her arm.*
(f) *Mary raised her consciousness.*

According to Schank, for each verb in the lexicon there is a list of
the possible primitives it can express. For instance, a word like *give*
would be defined as having at least two senses: 'transfer of
possession' (ATRANS) and 'transfer of mental information'
(MTRANS), as in *Mary gave some advice to John.*

Instead of specifying case frames for all the individual words in
the lexicon, Schank only needs to provide case frames for the
primitives. The case frames for ATRANS and MTRANS,
specifying appropriate values for the case slots, are shown opposite.
Note that in Schank's case frames the term 'Actor' is the equivalent
of the Agent case, and he uses Direction TO and FROM to
represent both the Recipient and Locative cases:

Actor: person
Act: ATRANS
Object: physical object
Direction TO: person
       FROM: person

Actor: person
Act: MTRANS
Object: information
Direction TO: person
       FROM: person

The beauty of primitives is that all verbs which involve the same primitive automatically have the same case frame. Thus the ATRANS case frame would be appropriate for all verbs implying transfer of possession, like *give*, *receive*, *take*, *buy*, *sell*. The MTRANS case frame would apply to all verbs for conveying information: e.g. *tell*, *inform*, and many others.

SAQ 21
Write a case frame for INGEST.

The appropriate primitive Act case frames for the 'strike' and 'collide' meanings of *hit* would be represented along the following lines:

'strike'
Actor: human (possibly using instrument)
Act: PROPEL
Object: physical object
Direction TO: physical object
       FROM: human

'collide'
Actor: none
Act: PTRANS
Object: at least two physical objects
Direction TO: each other
       FROM: unknown

You will find it instructive to compare this primitive Act case frame format with the other representations for 'strike' and 'collide': as semantic feature selection restrictions in Section 2.2; as case frames for verbs in Figure 2.3; and as predicates and arguments in Section 2.3. All of these formats represent the same information about possible subjects and objects, but the semantic primitives approach has the additional advantage that the case frame for 'strike' also applies to other verbs which involve applying force to a physical object (PROPEL).

Taken as lexical meanings of individual verbs, though, Schank's theory comes up against the same problems as other word definition theories. In particular, there is the difficulty of specifying the fine grain of which word combinations make sense, for instance, by listing all the objects which are 'giveable'; there is something very odd about *John gave Mary the Rocky Mountains*.

A second drawback is that to reduce words, e.g. *say*, *joke*, *preach*, *threaten*, *read*, to a single MTRANS primitive act obviously loses a lot of information. On the positive side, the use of primitives does make it possible to express similarities between all words which involve ATRANS, like *give*, *take*, *sell*, *buy*, or all words which involve INGEST, like *eat*, *breathe*, *drink*. This leads to an economy of selection restrictions: for instance, the constraints for all words for transferring mental information can be expressed just once for the primitive MTRANS, i.e. that they all require human Actors and Recipients.

2.5 Words and concepts

One question you might well be asking is whether features and case frames refer just to words or whether they are also relevant to the real-life concepts the words refer to. It certainly seems rather wasteful to postulate a set of semantic features or case frames for the words *ball*, *social assembly*, *give*, *admires* in the lexicon, and a whole other set of attributes for defining real-life entities like 'balls', 'giving' and 'admiring'.

We act towards balls as inanimate objects and would be astonished if they started talking to us. Even mythical objects like 'unicorns' or 'talking bears' in fairy stories are represented as concepts in memory. From this point of view, the lexicon and our knowledge of the world seem to be one and the same; in other words, our mental dictionary is identical to our mental encyclopaedia.

The implication of what I have said so far is that words are coined to reflect our concepts, both real and imaginary. However, a great deal of what we know depends on what people have told us. My concepts of 'freedom', 'cognitive psychology', 'right' and 'wrong' are shaped by what I have been told the words should mean. In another society my understanding of these words might be quite different. That is one reason why translation between languages is notoriously difficult.

The notion that it is language which shapes our thoughts rather than the other way round is known as *linguistic relativity*, the idea being that thoughts (i.e. our concepts) are not universal but are relative to the way our language defines them. This view is often known as the *Sapir-Whorf hypothesis* because it was first put forward in the 1920s and 1930s by a linguist Edward Sapir, and also by Benjamin Lee Whorf, a fire prevention engineer whose hobby was linguistics. You will find Whorf's ideas very interesting – a collection of his writings was published in 1956 (Whorf, 1956).

The current position on linguistic relativity is that the relationship between language and thought is a complex one. In many cases we derive concepts from real-life experiences first and are then told their names. In other cases, our concepts are totally dependent on linguistic definitions. Some perceptions, actions and feelings are so universal that most languages have terms for them, e.g. colours, movements, smiling. However, the way these basic reactions are interpreted may depend on social conventions, e.g. smiling may be considered friendly or a sign of weakness. These social conventions may have arisen from a mixture of economic and sociological factors, but they are perpetuated through language. For a further discussion of these fascinating topics see Cohen (1983).

Summary of Section 2

- The lexicon contains representations of word definitions which allow language users to select appropriate senses of words in sentence contexts.
- One way of defining words is in terms of semantic features like (+ physical object) (+ animal) (+ human). These features are used to express selection restrictions about permitted and non-permitted combinations of words.
- Another way of defining words is to formulate them as case frames which state the cases (Agent, Object, Instrument, etc.) which particular verbs require.

- A third way is to decompose word meanings into semantic primitives so that a single case frame requirement can be stated for all verbs which are examples of the same primitive Act, e.g. ATRANS (transfer of possession).
- According to the linguistic relativity hypothesis, thoughts are shaped by language, but the interaction between concepts and word definitions is a complex one which operates in both directions.

3   Syntactic processing

The message of the previous section was that it is not enough to know the meanings of individual words in order to understand sentences. In fact, it is very hard to define the meanings of many commonly used words, like *give* and *take*, without indicating the different meanings they could have in different sentence contexts. So in this section we shall be considering the role of grammatical combinations of words in understanding sentences.

3.1   Chomsky's theory of transformational grammar

Noam Chomsky is a linguist who has had a great influence on theories about the role of syntax in sentence understanding. He argues that our ability to recognize and understand grammatical English sentences is evidence that we must 'know' the rules of English grammar. For instance, anyone who knows English knows that *Colourless green ideas sleep furiously* is a grammatical sentence – although it is nonsense – while *Ideas green furiously colourless sleep* is ungrammatical.

SAQ 22
List at least one other combination of the words *ideas*, *green*, *furiously*, *colourless*, *sleep*, which makes a grammatical sentence.

Chomsky's theory is intended to formalize the rules which constitute linguistic competence: in other words, the knowledge which enables language speakers to identify some sequences of words as grammatical and others ungrammatical, as with the 'colourless ideas' example. Because it is a theory about competence, Chomsky's grammar says nothing about the actual processes people use to produce or understand sentences. Nevertheless, Chomsky's linguistic theory was the first to draw psychologists' attention to the syntactic rules of language. Before Chomsky (BC!), psychologists had mainly concentrated on the processing of single words, for the simple reason that they had no method for representing the structure of larger units like sentences and texts. Chomsky's demonstration that people are able to identify the 'grammaticality' of sentences was interpreted as supporting the idea that language processing involves parsing sentences into grammatical categories.

Chomsky's theory of grammar takes the form of rules for generating sentences. His use of the term *generative rules* has given rise to the mistaken view that Chomsky is postulating the rules language speakers actually use to produce utterances. Since Chomsky's is a competence theory, the term 'generating' is neutral about performance, being concerned only with the grammatical rules which distinguish between grammatical and ungrammatical combinations of words. A very simple example of some of the rules in Chomsky's grammar (1957) is shown in Figure 2.4.

1	S (sentence)	$\longrightarrow$	NP (noun phrase) + VP (verb phrase)
2	NP	$\longrightarrow$	N (noun)
3	NP	$\longrightarrow$	article + N
4	NP	$\longrightarrow$	adjective + N
5	NP	$\longrightarrow$	pronoun
6	VP	$\longrightarrow$	V (verb) + NP
7	VP	$\longrightarrow$	V + adjective
8	N	$\longrightarrow$	*Jane, boy, girl, apples*
9	V	$\longrightarrow$	*likes, hit, was hit, was, are cooking, are*
10	adjective	$\longrightarrow$	*good, unfortunate, cooking*
11	article	$\longrightarrow$	*a, the*
12	pronoun	$\longrightarrow$	*he, she, they*

Figure 2.4   Simplified version of Chomsky's rules (adapted from Greene, 1975)

These rules are known as *rewrite rules* because they rewrite a sentence into its constituent parts. According to Rule 1, the symbol for sentence (S) can be rewritten into symbols standing for noun phrase (NP) and verb phrase (VP). What this first rule is really saying is that sentences in English consist of a noun phrase followed by a verb phrase.

Rules 2–5 state that an NP can be rewritten either as an N (noun) e.g. *Jane*; or as an article plus N, e.g. *The boy*; or as an adjective plus N, e.g. *cooking apples*; or as a pronoun, e.g. *he*. Rules 6 and 7 state that a VP can be rewritten as a V (verb) and NP; or as a V and adjective. The NP introduced in Rule 6 can itself be rewritten according to Rules 2–5. Finally, Rules 8–12 allow the symbols to be rewritten as actual words. These rewrite rules can be used to produce *syntactic trees* which define the *syntactic structures* of sentences. For this reason the rules in Figure 2.4 are called *phrase structure rules*. An example of the way the rules can be used to generate a syntactic tree structure for a particular sentence is shown in Figure 2.5.

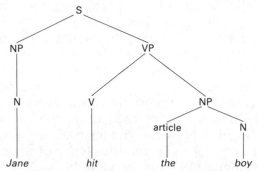

Figure 2.5   Syntactic tree structure

Syntactic tree structures show which of the rules have been used to generate a sentence. The symbols like NP, VP, N and so on are called the *nodes* of the tree. The rules keep being applied until all the symbols (nodes) are rewritten as actual words, known as the *terminal nodes* of the tree. For instance, the rules in Figure 2.4 used to generate the *Jane hit the boy* tree in Figure 2.5 are rules 1, 2, 6, 3, 8, 9, 11, 8. Make sure that you follow this example through, checking how each rule was used to rewrite a node in the syntactic tree.

SAQ 23
Using the grammar in Figure 2.4, draw a syntactic tree structure for the sentence *Jane was unfortunate*.

One great advantage of rewrite rules is that they can be used to specify different syntactic structures for sentences which have syntactically ambiguous structures. The sentence *They are cooking apples* can be analysed in two different ways, depending on whether it refers to two different types of apples, cooking or eating; or to the fact that people are cooking apples (see Figure 2.6).

On the other hand, the very simple rules in Figure 2.4 will generate quite a few ungrammatical word sequences. For instance, Rules 1, 2, 8, 6, 9, 2, 8 would generate the syntactic tree shown in Figure 2.7. Check that these rules do generate the tree in Figure 2.7.

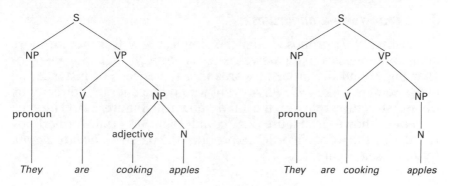

Figure 2.6   Syntactic structures of ambiguous sentence

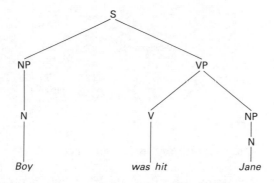

Figure 2.7   Syntactic structure of ungrammatical sequence

SAQ 24
Draw syntactic trees for the following word sequences:
(a) *They likes Jane*
(b) *Unfortunate was Jane*

The main reason why the grammar in Figure 2.4 generates ungrammatical sentences is because all the rules are *context free rules*, in the sense that each node can be rewritten independently of all the others. *Context dependent rules* place limitations on the rewrite rules so that the use of some of them is dependent on other rules. For instance, it could be specified that a V node must be rewritten as a plural verb if a plural NP has already been selected, ruling out the combination *they likes*. In other words, verbs have to be rewritten as plural in the context of a plural NP. However, it is more difficult to specify all the contexts in which the passive form of a verb should be selected, e.g. *was hit* in Figure 2.7.

69

3.2   *Transformational rules*

Chomsky (1957) proposed that the simplest way to generate more complex sentences like passives is to use *transformational rules* for changing round the order of words in a sentence. For instance, an active sentence like *Jane hit the boy* would be generated directly by phrase structure rules of the kind shown in Figure 2.4. The tree structure shown in Figure 2.5 could then be 'transformed' by reordering the words in order to produce the passive *The boy was hit by Jane* (see Figure 2.8).

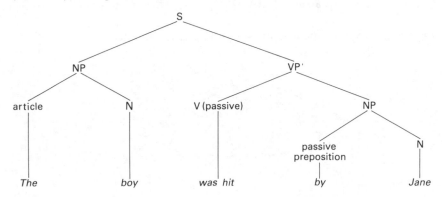

Figure 2.8   Syntactic structure of passive sentence

The passive transformation rule states that, when *Jane hit the boy* is transformed, the passive form of the verb (*was hit*) and the preposition *by* should be selected to produce *The boy was hit by Jane*. Transformational rules of this kind prevent the generation of ungrammatical sequences like *Boy was hit Jane*. This is because they specify how nodes should be rewritten taking into account the whole tree structure, rather than rewriting one node at a time. The idea is that the passive transformation can be applied to any active sentence with an NP + VP structure to turn it into its passive equivalent. Another advantage of transformational rules is that many interesting relationships between sentences can be expressed, e.g. that the first NP of a passive sentence like *The boy was hit by Jane* is always equivalent to the second NP of the equivalent active sentence *Jane hit the boy*.

In a later version of his theory, Chomsky (1965) made explicit the notion that each sentence has a *surface structure* and a *deep structure*. The surface structure represents the actual order of the words in a sentence, for instance, *The boy was hit by Jane*. The deep structure represents the basic grammatical relationships from which such a sentence is derived, i.e. *Jane hit the boy*.

The syntactic structure in Figure 2.8 represents the surface structure of *The boy was hit by Jane*, showing the *boy* as the subject of the verb. The syntactic structure in Figure 2.5 represents the deep structure for the same sentence, indicating that it is Jane who is doing the hitting. Chomsky reformulated transformational rules as rules for mapping deep structures on to surface structures, and vice versa.

SAQ 25
Which pairs of the sentences shown below have similar deep structures and which have similar surface structures?
(a) A new student painted the picture.
(b) The picture was painted by a new student.
(c) The picture was painted by a new technique.

Chomsky went on to suggest that deep structures contain all the syntactic information necessary for interpreting the meanings of sentences. Surface structures, on the other hand, are necessary for representing the words of a sentence in the correct order. A complete grammar must specify transformational rules for mapping surface structures on to deep structures and vice versa. Figure 2.9 shows the relationship between deep and surface structures in Chomsky's theory. You should note that there are no arrows shown between the boxes to emphasize that it is a model of linguistic competence which is 'neutral' about how language users actually process linguistic inputs.

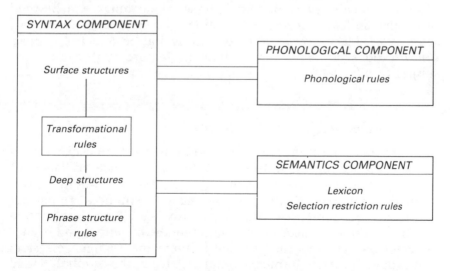

Figure 2.9   Chomsky's (1965) theory of language

The *Syntax component* consists of (a) phrase structure rules for generating deep structures and (b) transformational rules which map these deep structures on to surface structures. Surface structures feed into the *Phonological component* which contains phonological rules for generating the sounds of the words in the correct order. Deep structures provide all the syntactic information necessary for semantic analysis and are fed into the *Semantics component*.

An essential characteristic of Chomsky's model, as shown in Figure 2.9, is that the components are entirely separate. In particular, it is only after the rules in the Syntax component have fully completed the analysis of deep structures that they are input into the Semantics component. Chomsky's transformational grammar represents in its most extreme form the claim that syntax and semantics are quite distinct types of analysis.

The Semantics component contains rules for combining the meanings of words in acceptable combinations. The Syntax component can in principle generate all possible grammatical sentences, including nonsensical sentences like *Sincerity admires John* and *Colourless green ideas sleep furiously*. Although these sentences may conform to syntactic rules, they are *anomalous sentences* from the point of view of semantic interpretation. It was in order to rule out sentences like these that Katz and Fodor (1963) developed the theory of semantic features and selection restrictions discussed in Section 2.2. According to this theory, the Semantics component in Figure 2.9 would consist of a lexicon, defining the semantic features of words, and also rules for combining word meanings, which would bring into effect selection restrictions for rejecting anomalous sentences. Thus *Sincerity admires John* would be rejected because *sincerity* does not have the (+ human) feature required for the subject of *admires*.

3.3   Evaluation of Chomsky's theory

The first very important point to reiterate is that Chomsky's theory is intended to represent the linguistic competence of language speakers. The evidence relevant to his grammar is whether (a) it accounts for the generation of grammatical sentences, ruling out ungrammatical sentences, and (b) it provides all the information which is in principle necessary for relating the meanings and sounds of sentences. The fact that it is hard to imagine a language system that would generate sentences starting from the symbol S and working down to the actual words, or one that would generate grammatical sentences which would later be rejected by the Semantic component, is strictly irrelevant.

Chomsky believes that the type of rules formalized in transformational grammar constitute a universal grammatical competence which reflects the human ability to use language – although the actual syntactic rules and vocabulary of particular languages may result in many surface differences. Thus Chomsky's theory carries a strong implication that the rules of linguistic competence are represented in our brains and underlie our ability to produce and understand sentences. This notion that a knowledge of syntactic and semantic rules is responsible for people's ability to produce and understand language greatly influenced the way psychologists formulated models of language use.

In order to convert Figure 2.9 into an information processing model of language, psychologists only had to insert arrows between the boxes. For language comprehension, sentence inputs would first be analysed by the phonological rules into surface structures, then detransformed into deep structures, which would then be fed into the Semantics component for interpretation of sentence meanings. For production of sentences, the process would be reversed, starting with meanings, which are used to produce deep structures, which in turn are transformed into surface structures to be fed into the Phonological component for output as pronounced sounds. The implication of this model is that people have to carry out transformations and detransformations in order to produce and understand sentences.

This model gave rise to a lot of psychological research in the 1960s and 1970s. The term *psycholinguistics* was coined to emphasize the marriage between *psychology* and Chomsky's *linguistic* theory. Psycholinguists carried out experiments to test whether people's ability to memorize and evaluate the meanings of sentences is affected by the number and complexity of transformations needed to generate the sentences. For instance, Miller and McKean (1964) found that people take longer to transform a sentence like *Jane liked the boy* into the passive *The boy was liked by Jane* than into the negative *Jane did not like the boy*, while double transformations to the negative passive *The boy was not liked by Jane* took longest of all.

These results supported the theory that sentences are produced and understood by applying transformations. Perhaps this is not all that surprising since Miller and McKean actually asked their subjects to transform one type of sentence into another. However, other experiments revealed that, when people have to judge the meanings of sentences, they do not necessarily first carry out a transformational syntactic analysis and only then consider a semantic interpretation. An experiment demonstrating this is described in Techniques Box E.

TECHNIQUES BOX E

Slobin's Sentence Verification Experiment (1966)

Rationale
According to Chomsky's (1957) theory, active sentences (A) require no transformations, passive sentences (P) require a single passive transformation to reorder the words, negatives (N) require a single negative transformation, and passive negative (PN) sentences require two transformations. It was predicted that subjects would take longer to evaluate sentences requiring more transformations.

Method
Sentences of various types were presented to subjects (Ss) along with a picture (see examples below). The sentences had to be judged as true (T) or false (F) depending on how they described the scene in the picture, known as a *sentence verification task*.

Sentence	Picture
The girl is watering the flowers. (A)	Girl watering flowers(T)
The dog is being chased by the cat. (P)	Dog chasing cat(F)
The girl is not watering the flowers. (N)	Girl watering flowers(F)
The cat is not being chased by the dog. (PN)	Cat chasing dog(T)

Some of the sentences were called 'reversible' because the subject and object could be reversed and still result in a sensible sentence, e.g. *The dog is chasing the cat* or *The cat is chasing the dog*. Other sentences were 'irreversible' because switching the subject and object resulted in a nonsensical sentence, e.g. *The flowers are watering the girl*.

Results
Reaction times to verify true sentences (seconds)

	A	P	N	PN
Reversible	0.93	1.21	1.27	1.75
Irreversible	0.70	0.69	0.98	1.01

As you can see from the table, in general A sentences were verified most quickly while PN sentences took the longest times. However, a surprising finding was that, with the irreversible sentences, Ss took no longer to judge the irreversible passive *The flowers are being watered by the girl* than the equivalent irreversible active *The girl is watering the flowers*, despite the fact that the passive is supposed to need an extra transformation. With reversible sentences subjects did take longer to judge passives than actives.

Slobin interpreted the finding that irreversible passives are relatively easy as demonstrating that the semantic implausibility of flowers watering girls offsets the syntactic complexity of a passive transformation. These findings, and other similar results, cast doubt on the contention that syntactic analysis into deep structures must be completed before the Semantics component can start work. People make assumptions about what a sentence might plausibly mean and, indeed, may sometimes bypass syntactic analysis altogether, e.g. assuming that it must be the girl who is doing the watering.

SAQ 26
Which of these sentences (taken from Herriot, 1969) should subjects find easy or difficult?
(a) *The doctor treated the patient.*
(b) *The boy was kissed by the girl.*
(c) *The lifeguard was saved by the bather.*

Since 1965 Chomsky has continued to dominate linguistics in the sense that even linguists who think of themselves as anti-Chomsky have implicitly accepted his views about the aims of a linguistic theory. As a result of considering many examples and counter-examples of English sentences, in later versions of his theory Chomsky (1980) recognized that the surface structures of sentences contain linguistic cues about appropriate deep structures, e.g. the *by* in passive sentences. Consequently, Chomsky suggested that, instead of deep structures containing all the information necessary for semantic analysis, an abstract form of surface structure, which contains *traces* of transformational reorderings, may contain sufficient information for input to the Semantics component. Chomsky's later reformulations of transformational grammar are of great interest to linguists but have had little impact on psychological theories of language.

Moreover, Chomsky continues to ignore psychological evidence that people do not wait for a complete syntactic analysis before

75

starting to hazard guesses about what a sentence means, relegating such matters to 'mere' performance. As a result, many psychologists have very mixed feelings about the influence of Chomsky's theory on psychology. In fact, it is fashionable to decry Chomsky as being only interested in the syntax of sentences rather than the more interesting topic of sentence meanings. It must be said in Chomsky's defence that it was transformational grammar that first alerted psychologists to the complexities involved in language use and led directly to experiments which demonstrate that all sorts of factors are implicated in semantic interpretations.

The major legacy of Chomsky's theory is that most models of language incorporate mapping rules for extracting some kind of 'deep' representations from the surface forms of sentences. As we shall see in later sections, the types of rules range from syntactic parsers, closely based on the rules of Chomsky's grammar, to semantic rules which exploit semantic and/or general knowledge to derive meanings directly. All models, though, have to make some allowance for the ordering of words and other grammatical indicators which make up the syntax of a language; they have to cope in one way or another with the syntactic parsing problem.

3.4   Syntactic parsers (ATNs)

Many models of language incorporate a *syntactic parser* which scans the words in a sentence in order to build up a tree structure of syntactic constituents. These syntactic constituents are very like those in Chomsky's transformational grammar: NP (noun phrase), VP (verb phrase), etc. Moreover, the parsing rules essentially perform the same functions as the rewrite rules in defining the syntactic structures of grammatical sentences.

However, there is one big difference between Chomsky's rewrite rules and these parsers. A grammar specifies *what* the rewrite rules are (competence) whereas a parser specifies *how* to use these rules to analyse a sentence (performance). In addition, many parsers have the aim of modelling the actual processes used by language users. They do this by operating in a left to right fashion, making hypotheses about grammatical structures as they go along. The assumption is that people also take in the sounds or written words of a sentence from left to right – at least in English.

Perhaps the most commonly used type of syntactic *parser* is based on a formalism known as *Augmented Transition Networks (ATNs)*, first developed by Woods (1970). They are called *transition networks* because they look at transitions between each of the constituents of a sentence, starting at the beginning and working through the sentence from left to right. Transition networks take the form of a series of *states* with arrows (called *arcs*) which link one state to the next. Let us start by looking at how a transition network would represent the first rule of Chomsky's grammar in Figure 2.4, stating that a sentence (S) is made up of a NP and a VP. This is shown in Figure 2.10 (a).

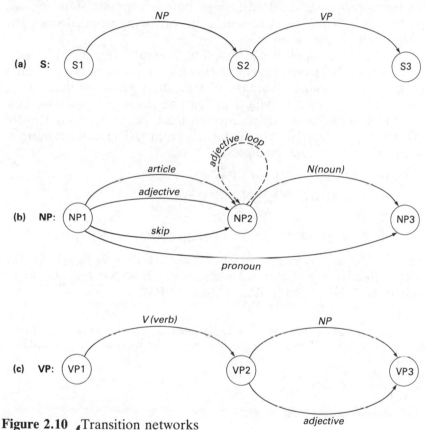

Figure 2.10 Transition networks

The arcs in transition networks are labelled to indicate the rules which allow the grammar to move from one state to the next. In Figure 2.10 (a), the parser can only proceed from state (S1) to state (S2) if it can 'find' an NP. From state (S2) it can only finish the sentence by moving to state (S3) if the next constituent it finds is a VP.

But how can the parser go about finding an NP? A transition network which encapsulates all the ways an NP can be rewritten (according to Rules 2–5 in Figure 2.4) is shown in Figure 2.10 (b).

Starting from state (NP1), the rules for proceeding to (NP2) require an article or an adjective. The *skip arc* expresses the fact that, according to Rule 2 in Figure 2.4, it is possible to complete an NP by going straight to the N (noun) arc. Rule 5 allows an NP to consist of a pronoun on its own; therefore there has to be an arc which goes straight to state (NP3) if the parser comes across a pronoun. Finally, there is an adjective 'loop' in Figure 2.10 (b) which captures the fact that there can be several adjectives before a noun, as in *big red square block*. This loop arc would go on being applied until the parser comes across a noun.

This ability to allow for a 'loop' of several adjectives is a new feature of the NP transition network which was not in the grammar in Figure 2.4. It is an advantage of transition networks that all the possible arcs from a particular state can be easily grouped together. Thus there are several 'paths' through the arcs and states in the NP network in Figure 2.10 (b), all starting from (NP1) and finishing at (NP3). Here are some examples:

(NP1) article (NP2) N (NP3)

(NP1) adjective (NP2) N (NP3)

(NP1) skip (NP2) N (NP3)

(NP1) article (NP2) adjective loop (NP2) N (NP3)

The NP *The big blocks* would be analysed as: (NP1) article *The* (NP2) adjective *big* (NP2) N *blocks* (NP3). The NP *Jane* would be analysed as: (NP1) skip (NP2) N *Jane* (NP3).

SAQ 27
List the states and labelled arcs that would need to be followed through the NP network in Figure 2.10 (b) for the following noun phrases (or write 'impossible' if no suitable series of transitions will work):
(a) *The boy*
(b) *Big blue blocks*
(c) *She*
(d) *The tall and bright child.*

To complete the syntactic rules for completing an NP + VP sentence, we need a transition network to specify the constituents of a VP as shown in Figure 2.10 (c). Taken together, the transition networks (a), (b) and (c) in Figure 2.10 specify the rules for parsing a whole sentence. The parser works by going through the transition networks; at each transition it tries to find a constituent or word which will allow it to follow one of the labelled arcs. When it has completed all the arcs in any one network the parser reports back its successful search. The parsing process can then proceed until a sentence is completely parsed.

The parsing process starts with the S network in Figure 2.10 (a). In order to proceed from state (S1) to state (S2) the parser has to find an NP. To achieve this the parser moves down to the NP network in (b) to follow the arcs necessary to find an NP. Assuming that it has identified an NP and reached (NP3), the parser can report back to state (S2) in the S network in (a). The next instruction to the parser is to find a VP to finish the sentence. The parser starts working its way through the VP network in (c). When it has found a verb to reach (VP2), it either follows the adjective arc or it is sent back to (b) to look for another NP. When this is finished the parser reports back to the VP network which can then move on to (VP3). Finally, the parser reports back to the S network in (a) that it has found a VP and the parser moves to (S3) to complete the sentence.

This may seem a bit clearer if we follow the parsing of a particular sentence through the transition networks. Let us take as an example our old friend *Jane hit the boy*. The parsing would proceed as follows through the states and labelled arcs in Figure 2.10:

> (S1) find NP (NP1) skip (NP2) N *Jane* (NP3) NP finished (S2) find VP (VP1) V *hit* (VP2) find NP (NP1) article *the* (NP2) N *boy* (NP3) NP finished (VP3) VP finished (S3) sentence finished.

SAQ 28
Make a list of the states and labelled arcs in the (a), (b), and (c) networks in Figure 2.10 which would be needed to parse the following sentence: *Jane was unfortunate.*

I hope this has given you a feel for how syntactic parsers operate. Of course, just like the simple example of Chomsky's rules in Figure 2.4, transition networks would have to incorporate a much greater choice of arcs to allow for the analysis of more complex sentences. What attracted researchers to transition networks was their formalization of grammatical rules as left to right transitions. As a performance model, the labelled arcs in transition networks can be thought of as providing rules for testing each word as it comes in to see whether it fits into a particular syntactic structure.

There is, however, one major problem with all left to right parsers. This is the question of how they know which of all the alternative arcs they should choose to follow from each state. The sentences we have discussed so far pose no difficulty since there is only one way in which they can be parsed. But what about a sentence like *They are cooking apples*, which can either be parsed as (NP) *They* (V) *are* (NP) *cooking apples* or (NP) *They* (V) *are cooking* (NP) *apples*? The parser would start off by deciding that *They* is a possible NP. But when it comes to the words *are* and *cooking*, how would it know whether to treat *are* or *are cooking* as a V or whether *cooking* is an adjective?

Quite often the syntax of sentences cannot be decided until later on in a sentence. For instance, the words *The building blocks* can be completed as *The building blocks are red*, or *The building blocks the sun*, or even *The building blocks the sun faded are red*. In the first and last sentences the words *The building blocks* should be classified as a NP; in the second sentence as a NP plus V.

The question which exercises researchers is what action a syntactic parser should take when it is faced with the possibility of several different ways of analysing a sentence by following alternative arcs. There are several ways in which such a parser could operate:

1 The parser could compute all possibilities at each word transition, i.e. *The building blocks* would be identified as both a complete NP and as a NP plus V. If the next word is *are*, the NP route is confirmed. The problem is that there are just too many possibilities for even a computer program to keep track of. If the next words after *The building blocks* turn out to be *the sun*, this might be either the end of a sentence, or the beginning of a relative clause, i.e. *The building blocks (which) the sun faded*.

2 The parser could plump for the most probable grammatical structure, e.g. *The building blocks* as an NP. But, if it later comes across words like *the sun*, it could *backup* to an earlier transition point in order to take another arc through the network, this time identifying *The building* as a complete NP on its own followed by the verb *blocks*.

3 The parser could *look ahead* to see what is coming next before deciding how to analyse the current transition. If it sees the words *are red* coming up it can safely identify *The building blocks* as an NP.

4 The parser could call on other components like the semantics component to see whether *The building* or *The building blocks* is the most likely interpretation of the sentence in that particular context.

ATNs are called *augmented* transition networks because they have the facility to suspend judgement about a group of words by putting them into a temporary store, called a *register*, while they look ahead or consult other components as necessary. These registers allow them to take context into account before deciding which arc to take through the grammar network.

A good example of the use of registers is the parsing of passive sentences like *The boy was hit by Jane*. The first NP *The boy* would be held in a register as the potential subject of the sentence. A more sophisticated version of the VP network would take account of whether verbs are in the active, like *hit*, or in the passive form, *was hit*. When the parser comes across a passive verb, plus the preposition *by*, the contents of the 'subject' register can be changed, substituting *Jane* for *The boy*. This ability to change the contents of registers, depending on which arcs are activated, gives ATNs the power to represent *Jane* as the 'true' subject of *hit*. This is exactly equivalent to Chomsky's passive transformation rule, which related the surface structure of *The boy was hit by Jane* with its deep structure *Jane hit the boy*. Another example of the use of registers is when a plural NP like *They* is held in a register until the parser finds a plural verb, thus preventing the parser from selecting a structure like *They likes Jane*.

It is because of their ability to specify complicated rules, which interrelate the contents of registers and the parsing of the rest of the sentence, that Augmented Transition Networks have proved so effective for parsing sentences. Working in a left to right direction, they allow for decisions to be altered in the light of transitions taken later in a sentence. This means that context can be taken into account when deciding on the appropriate analysis of a sentence.

Summary of Section 3

- Chomsky's transformational grammar specifies the syntactic rules which reflect linguistic competence, as demonstrated by speakers' ability to distinguish between grammatical and ungrammatical sentences.
- The Syntax component contains two types of rules: phrase structure rules, which generate deep structures, and transformational rules, which map deep structures and surface structures on to each other.
- In Chomsky's 1965 theory, deep structures contain the syntactic information necessary for interpretation by the Semantics component. Surface structures contain the syntactic information necessary for the Phonological component to represent the sounds of words in the correct order. The three components in Chomsky's theory are independent, allowing for no interaction between syntactic and semantic analysis.
- Psycholinguists interpreted Chomsky's 1965 theory as an information processing model for the production and comprehension of sentences. However, experiments showed that people do not complete a full syntactic analysis of sentences before starting to interpret meanings.

- Syntactic parsers are often formulated as Augmented Transition Networks (ATNs) which build up syntactic structures by looking at transition arcs between states in a left to right direction. The use of registers for holding sentence constituents enables the parser to take into account the developing structure of a sentence.

4   *Semantic processing*

In Section 3 we discussed the syntactic rules for the grammatical analysis of sentences. However, there are many language researchers who would deny the need for a separate syntactic component. They argue that it is much simpler to go straight from the words in a sentence to semantic representations. Syntactic parsers aim to analyse sentences into syntactic constitutents like NP and VP; semantic analysers aim to analyse sentences directly into semantic categories like Actor and Object.

4.1   *Semantic analysers*

If you look back to Section 2.4, you will see that Schank proposed that word meanings are defined by specifying the case frames into which they can fit. According to Schank, language processing takes the form of rules which test whether each word in a sentence is a likely candidate for the case slots of the main verb. Like syntactic parsers, semantic analysers look at words in a left to right direction. For the sentence *The big boy gave Mary some advice* the semantic analyser would carry out tests along the following lines:

1 Is the first NP human? If so, assign it (*The big boy*) as the Actor of the verb.
2 Which primitive Act is most likely to be associated with the verb? In this case ATRANS (transfer of possession) is the most likely candidate for *give*. This leads the model to expect an Object and a human Recipient (i.e. Direction TO).
3 Is the next NP human? If so, assign it (*Mary*) to the Direction TO slot.
4 Is the next NP a physical object? No; as *advice* is a mental entity rather than a physical object, recategorize *give* as MTRANS (transfer of mental information).

5 Recheck that human Actors and Recipients are appropriate for
   MTRANS. If so, output semantic representation of the sentence
   as:

> Actor: *big boy*
>
> Act: MTRANS
>
> Object: *advice*
>
> Direction TO: *Mary*
>
> FROM: *big boy*

SAQ 29
Fill in the slots required to represent the meaning of the sentence *Jane kicked the
ball through the window*. HINT: Look back to Schank's Acts listed in Section 2.4.

Of course, as you have probably noticed, some syntactic information still has to be taken into account in deciding what constitutes
an NP like *The big boy*. Equally, if a verb is passive as in *The book
was given to Mary by John*, new rules would be needed to assign the
NPs *Mary* and *John* to the Actor and Recipient slots. However,
there is one important difference between semantic analysers and
syntactic parsers. Both have to take into account grammatical rules
about word order, and whether verbs are active or passive, whether
nouns are singular or plural. But the whole purpose of syntactic
parsers is to represent this kind of grammatical information. In
contrast, semantic analysers only consider syntactic information
when necessary in order to decide on semantic categories. Another
way of expressing this distinction is to say that syntactic parsers are
syntactically driven parsers whereas semantic analysers are *semantically driven parsers*.

Presented with the passive sentence *The book was given to Mary
by John*, a semantic analyser would allocate the word *book* to the
Object slot on semantic considerations alone as being the only non-
human noun in the sentence. A syntactic parser would have no way
of knowing whether *the book* is a likely NP candidate for the object
of *give*. The advantage of semantic analysers is that syntactic and
semantic information is completely intertwined. This is in contrast
to language understanding systems in which there are separate
syntactic and semantic components.

However, it is possible for semantic parsers to start by allocating a
semantic interpretation and find that it is incorrect as the sentence
progresses. This is equivalent to the problems faced by syntactic
parsers when there is more than one possible syntactic structure for
the first words in a sentence. Semantic analysers work by selecting
the most probable candidates for case frame slots, changing their
semantic interpretation if required by later words in the sentence.

This method of operation is borne out by the fact that people are sometimes surprised by the way a sentence ends: for instance, *The shooting of the prince shocked his wife because she thought he was an excellent marksman* (Foss and Hakes, 1978). Sentences which require a semantic reinterpretation halfway through are called *garden path sentences*, because they lead the listener up the garden path before revealing the correct interpretation.

4.2   Conceptual Dependency representations

The next question to consider is what kind of semantic representations of a sentence emerge as a result of semantic processing. Not surprisingly, such representations reflect the case frames which have been filled in by the semantic analyser. Schank called the sentence representations resulting from semantic analysis *Conceptual Dependencies (CDs)*. He used this term because the sentence representations show the way in which the concepts referred to in the sentence depend on each other. In addition to case representations for single actions, CD analysis can also show causal relations between actions and states. Thus the sentence *John hurt Mary* would be represented as:

Actor: *John*
Act: unknown
Object: unknown
    CAUSED
State: *hurt*
Object: *Mary*

The point of representing sentences as frames with slots is that it sets up expectations to help the semantic analyser to interpret new inputs such as *John was sorry so he stopped hitting Mary*. From this the inference could be made that the unknown slot for Act might be filled by MOVE and the Object by *fist* in the direction TO Mary FROM John. In other words, CDs allow inferences to be made which go beyond the literal meanings of sentences.

Another notation for Conceptual Dependencies you may come across in the literature is a form of semantic network which Schank used in his earlier work (1972). Some typical examples are shown in Figure 2.11.

These networks are exactly equivalent to the CD frames already presented. The conventions for representing the slots for Actor, Object and Direction TO/FROM are shown in the key to Figure 2.11. Check for yourselves that (a) in Figure 2.11 represents exactly

(a)   *big boy* $\Longleftrightarrow$ MTRANS $\xleftarrow{\;\circ\;}$ *advice* $\underset{\Large\diagdown}{\overset{\Large\diagup}{\vert}}$ $\rightarrow$ *Mary*
$\langle$ *big boy*

(b)   *Mary gave a book to John*

A book was given by Mary to John , etc.

Mary $\Longleftrightarrow$ ATRANS $\xleftarrow{\;\circ\;}$ *book* $\underset{\Large\diagdown}{\overset{\Large\diagup}{\vert}}$ $\rightarrow$ *John*
$\langle$ *Mary*

(c)   *Bill told Mary that John gave him a book*

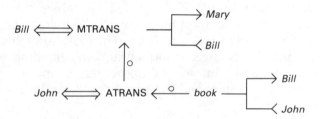

(d)   *Mary sold John a book*

John bought a book from Mary , etc.

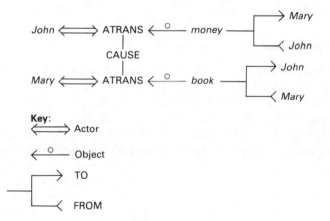

Key:

$\xLongleftrightarrow{\quad}$ Actor

$\xleftarrow{\;\circ\;}$ Object

$\rightarrow$ TO

$\langle$ FROM

Figure 2.11   Conceptual Dependency networks

the same information given in the CD for *The big boy gave Mary some advice* in Section 4.1.

Schank makes the point that Conceptual Dependencies represent semantic relationships between real-life events rather than syntactic relationships between words. Consequently, all sentences which refer to the same real-life situation would be mapped on to the same Conceptual Dependency network. For instance, the CD in Figure 2.11(b) represents the conceptual meaning of a whole set of sentences like *John was given a book by Mary, Mary gave John a book* and *A book was given to John by Mary*.

It is also possible to use two or more CDs to represent the meaning of more complex sentences. Example (c) in Figure 2.11 represents *Bill told Mary that John gave him a book*. The Object slot of what Bill told (MTRANS) Mary is filled in by the whole of the statement about John giving (ATRANS) a book to Bill. In this way one CD can be embedded into another to show semantic inter-relationships between sentences.

The final example (d) in Figure 2.11 shows the CD which represents the meaning of sentences like *John bought the book from Mary* and *Mary sold the book to John*. The CD shows the causal link between a prior exchange of money and the handing over of the book. It also allows inferences to be made about who was in possession of the money and the book before and after the sale.

SAQ 30
Draw conceptual dependency networks to represent the following sentences:
(a) *John gave Mary a dog.*
(b) *As a result of Mary's advice John gave her a lift home.*
HINT: Relevant Acts for (b) are MTRANS and PTRANS.

4.3   Propositions

Another way of representing semantic meanings is as *propositions*. These use exactly the same *predicate calculus* notation introduced in Section 2.3 as a method of representing verbs as predicates and case slots as arguments. It would be a good idea if you looked back to that section now and checked the answer to SAQ 19. Using this notation, each sentence is represented as a main verb (predicate) plus slots for the cases (arguments). *Mary gave the book to John* would be represented by a proposition in which the verb *gave* is followed by case argument slots which have been filled in with particular words. In addition we can give the whole proposition a label such as Proposition–1 so that we can refer back to it later:

                                    Agent   Object   Recipient
          Proposition–1: *gave* (*Mary*,   *book*,   *John*)

This exactly mirrors the information given in the CD in Figure 2.11 (b) (Actor and Agent are of course equivalent, as are Recipient and Direction TO). In fact, propositions are simply a notational device for representing case relationships between words in a convenient way. They are particularly useful for showing relationships within sentences – or between several sentences – when semantic networks can become rather over-complex and difficult to 'read'. For instance, propositions can easily be embedded into each other to represent a sentence like *Bill told Mary that John gave him a book:*

Proposition–1: *told* (*Bill*, Proposition–2, *Mary*)
Proposition–2: *gave* (*John*, *book*, *Bill*)

This means that the whole of Proposition–2 gets inserted as the Object of what Bill told Mary, namely that John gave him (Bill) a book. Take enough time with this example until you are sure you see why this is exactly equivalent to (c) in Figure 2.11. Note that in propositions the verb is always given first because all the cases relate to the verb.

SAQ 31
List the propositions in the following sentence?

  The teacher said John broke the window.

While Conceptual Dependencies and propositions can in principle be used as equivalent notations, there is a general tendency for researchers who analyse sentences into propositions to concentrate on the actual words in sentences rather than breaking them down (i.e. decomposing) them into semantic primitives like ATRANS and PTRANS. Van Dijk and Kintsch (1983) argue that people do not always need to decompose propositions into primitives in order to understand sentences. They point out that readers can understand a proposition like *hurt (John, Mary)* directly, without breaking *hurt* down further to produce two propositions representing the causal relation that John must have performed some Act which caused Mary to be in a hurt state. What the difference really comes down to is the question of how many causal inferences about what is happening need to be included in sentence representations. As we shall see in Part III, this issue is a very important one for models of language understanding.

4.4   Syntax or semantics?

As you must have realized by now, theories about language processing go hand in hand with theories about how meanings are represented. Everyone agrees, of course, that the final aim of language processing is to represent meanings. The question at issue is whether there is an identifiable separate stage of syntactic parsing, the output of which is a syntactic tree structure showing grammatical relations between words. Supporters of the syntactic position postulate that at some stage during the extraction of meanings from linguistic inputs, the parser will produce a syntactic representation which represents the grammatical structure of sentences in terms of constituents like NP, VP, etc.

Those who take the semantic position deny the need for a separate stage of syntactic parsing. Instead they believe that syntactic and semantic information are processed simultaneously in order to derive semantic representations of sentence meanings. Any reference to grammatical indicators will be 'driven' by the need to extract conceptual representations of the situations described by sentences.

Ritchie and Thompson (1984) give amusing caricatures of how the semantic approach (which they call *asyntactic*) and the syntactic approach would tackle a potentially ambiguous sentence like *Robin banks with Barclays*:

> A caricature of the asyntactic (i.e. semantic) position proceeds as follows:
> My dictionary tells me that this string of characters either refers to the edges of bodies of water, to financial institutions, or to the process of using a financial institution. Similarly, it tells me that *Robin* refers to a human, and *Barclays* to a particular financial institution. There is only one sensible way of combining these meanings into a single coherent meaning – The human named Robin uses the financial institution named Barclays.
> A caricature of the syntactic position would be:
> My dictionary tells me that *Robin* is a proper noun, *banks* either a plural noun or the third person singular of a verb, *with* a preposition and *Barclays* another proper noun. My grammar tells me that well-formed utterances in English can consist of the sequence proper noun, verb, preposition, proper noun but that the sequence proper noun, noun, preposition, proper noun is not a well-formed English utterance. Therefore *banks* is in this case a verb.

As Ritchie and Thompson go on to point out, both approaches have advantages and disadvantages. The first takes us nearer to the actual meaning of the sentence but the second is much less vague about the way the rules should be applied. The semantic analysis depends on knowing the 'only one sensible way of combining these meanings into a single coherent meaning'. Humans are able to do this easily but it is clear that we don't yet know enough about how they do it to specify the exact operations which should be incorporated into a model. The position is, unfortunately, not much better when we turn to the results of experiments designed to test whether people actually use syntactic or semantic representations. One common technique, which was introduced in Part I, is to test memory for sentences. It is known that people tend to recall the meanings of sentences rather than exact wordings. Therefore, testing people's memory for linguistic inputs should reveal something about how they represent the meanings of sentences.

In most experiments, sentence representations are inferred from *recognition confusions*. If subjects are unable to tell the difference between one version of a sentence, which they actually read or heard, and another version, which is in fact a 'new' sentence, it is assumed that the subject's representation of the original sentence cannot have included the kind of information necessary to distinguish the two versions. For instance, suppose people are not sure whether they heard *John gave Mary the book* or *Mary was given the book by John*. The argument is that their mental representations cannot have reflected the surface forms of these two sentences (which are quite different) but must represent their very similar deep structures, i.e. *John gave the book to Mary*, which might easily become confused. Equally, if people confuse sentences which have different deep structures but the same meanings, it can be concluded that they represent sentences as meanings rather than deep structures. A typical experiment of this kind is described in Techniques Box F.

TECHNIQUES BOX F

Johnson-Laird and Stevenson's Experiment (1970)

Rationale
It was predicted that subjects would confuse sentences with the same meanings, even when the sentences have different deep structures.

Method
Subjects were presented with a tape-recorded passage of text including sentences like (a) *John liked the painting and bought it from the duchess.* Later subjects had to recognize a sentence like this from a list of other sentences which had not been previously presented, including sentences like (b) *The painting pleased John and the duchess sold it to him.*

Results
Subjects tended to select new sentences like (b) as one of the sentences they thought they had originally been presented with, showing that they had confused the two versions.

Johnson-Laird (1974) interpreted these results as demonstrating that syntactic deep structures are not a necessary level of representation. According to Chomsky's theory, *The painting pleased John* and *John liked the painting* have different deep structures. While *John liked the painting* and *The painting was liked by John* have similar deep structures, a purely syntactic theory cannot reflect the semantic relationship between the words *liked* and *pleased*. So, as far as syntax is concerned, there is no relationship between the sentences *John liked the painting* and *The painting pleased John*. Obviously what links the sentences about John, the painting, and the duchess is that they would all be given the same semantic representation. So this experiment supports the idea that people remember semantic rather than syntactic representations.

SAQ 32
(a) How would the sentences *John bought the painting from the duchess* and *The duchess sold the picture to John* be represented as Conceptual Dependency networks? HINT: Look back to Figure 2.11 (d).
(b) Would Schank predict that subjects would tend to confuse the representations for these two sentences?

The findings from many experiments like Johnson-Laird's certainly show that subjects tend to remember the gist of sentences rather than exact wordings. One problem with this line of experimentation is that no-one doubts that people eventually extract meaningful representations from what they hear or read. But at the actual time when they are processing utterances, people have to take into account syntactic surface structure information, such as whether a sentence is active or passive, uses a question or imperative construction, etc. It has not so far proved possible to design experiments which will 'catch' language understanders at each stage of processing. The results of language processing are stored in memory rather than the processes themselves, or any intermediate stages of representation. This unfortunately makes it rather difficult to test theories about syntactic and semantic representations on the basis of psychological experiments. Other methods for evaluating theories of language understanding will be discussed in Part III.

Summary of Section 4

- In contrast to theories incorporating a separate syntactic parser, semantic theories claim that syntactic and semantic analysis is an indivisible process.
- Schank's model includes a semantic analyser which tests the words in a sentence from left to right to see whether they are

likely candidates to fill slots for semantic categories, such as Actor, Act, Object and Recipient.

- The resulting Conceptual Dependency (CD) representations of sentences reflect conceptual relationships based on the real-life situations described by sentences.
- Propositions can also be used to represent sentence meanings as verbs (predicates) and case slots (arguments).
- Experiments show that people remember semantic interpretations rather than syntactic structures. While these findings appear to support semantic theories, they do not conclusively prove that syntactic processing does not occur at any stage. What they do show is that syntactic and semantic processes are interactive rather than being separate components.

5   Discourse processing

So far we have been considering representations of individual sentences. But, of course, most of what we read consists of longer passages of texts, newspaper articles, textbooks, instruction manuals, encyclopaedias, short stories, novels and biographies. So, even supposing that we knew exactly how sentences are represented, we would still need to ask how language users put all these meanings together in order to appreciate the meaning of a whole text.

This level of analysis is called *textual linguistics* or *discourse analysis*. There are two major topics considered under this heading. The first is *local coherence*, which is concerned with ways in which references between adjacent sentences are understood. The second investigates the *global structure* of a whole text.

5.1   Local coherence

One of the main factors in achieving local coherence between adjoining sentences is deciding what pronouns refer to. This is known as *anaphoric reference*. Some of these references are signalled by syntactic cues. For instance, in the sentence *When he came into the library John spoke to Jim*, the *he* must refer to *John*. But, in the sentence *John spoke to Jim when he came into the library* the *he* can refer to either *John* or *Jim*.

Clark and Clark (1977) point out there are many occasions when semantic considerations override syntactic rules. For instance, in the sentence *When the Clarks saw the Rocky Mountains flying across the country they realized how beautiful they were*, there is no ambiguity about what the two *theys* refer to – we also make the inference that it is the Clarks not the Rockies who are 'flying'. Van Dijk and Kintsch (1983) list several of the factors which may affect pronoun reference and describe a rather ingenious experimental technique for testing the references people select for pronouns (see Techniques Box G).

TECHNIQUES BOX G

Van Dijk and Kintsch's Pronoun Reference Technique (1983)

Rationale
Given that a preceding sentence allows a choice of pronoun references, people will select the reference which is the topic of the previous sentence, i.e. the given information to which any new information refers.

Method
Subjects were presented with sentences followed by a second sentence starting with a pronoun which subjects could complete as they liked. From their sentence completions it was possible to judge which of the nouns in the first sentence they had used the pronoun to refer to. Sentences were chosen so that sometimes the topic noun was at the beginning of the sentence and sometimes not. Examples – with the topic noun shown in bold – are:
(a) *The **director** fired a worker. He . . .*
(b) *To a passing lady **Josie** gave away her fur coat. She . . .*

Results
In general, subjects completed sentences so that the pronoun referred to the topic of the preceding sentence, e.g. for sentence (a) a typical continuation was *He was known to be a tough boss*; for sentence (b) *She wished she had kept it for herself*. However, other factors, like whether a character was referred to by a proper name, or the position of the topic noun in the preceding sentence, also had an effect on pronoun selections.

Van Dijk and Kintsch quote these results as showing that people interpret sentences in order to maintain topical coherence. But as Clark and Murphy (1982) point out, it is not always so obvious what a pronoun or noun refers to, because there may have been no direct mention of the previous topic. With a pair of sentences like *Jean had a bruise on his cheek. Mary did it*, the listener has to make a bridging inference that the pronoun *it* refers to some action by Mary which caused a bruise (see examples of bridging inferences in Part I, Sections 3.1 and 3.2). Other kinds of local coherence between sentences involve causal inferences. For instance, the sentences *John was murdered yesterday. The knife lay nearby*, would be interpreted as meaning that someone performed an action with the knife which caused the state of John being dead. The kinds of inferences readers make to achieve local coherence are known as *elaborative inferences*, because they *add* connections which are not stated in the original text.

5.2   Global structure

Global structure refers to the overall interpretation of a text. Since most people cannot remember the actual wording of long texts, they recall only the *gist*, leaving out less important details. Van Dijk and Kintsch (1983) call this the *macrostructure* of a text. In contrast to the *elaborative inferences* made at the level of local coherence, when they are reading longer texts readers have to make *reductive inferences* which will reduce the text to a much shorter and manageable summary of the main points.

Van Dijk and Kintsch (1983) proposed a model of discourse processing which involves extracting *macropropositions* from an initial analysis of individual sentences into propositions (see Section 4.3). However, macropropositions do not simply connect up successive propositions for individual sentences; rather they depend on inferences about which topics are central to the main theme in order to build up a macrostructure for the whole text. In the process of doing this, readers make use of knowledge about the content of the text, the message it may be trying to convey, and the type of text it is – folk-tale, newspaper article, experimental novel or boring textbook. All the different types of general knowledge discussed in earlier sections, including scripts and story schemas, can be brought to bear on building up a macrostructure for a particular text.

The extraction of macrostructures is an ongoing process in language understanding. Far from waiting until the end of a text to decide what it was all about, readers continuously make inferences about relevant macropropositions. Moreover, macropropositions have a great deal of influence on how the rest of a text is analysed. If a reader decides that the point of a newspaper article is to discuss the causes of a strike, he or she may well ignore sentence propositions which do not seem to fit in with this theme. Readers gradually narrow down text representations to more and more global macropropositions. The final set of macropropositions represents the macrostructure of the text as it will be stored in memory.

One method for studying macrostructures is to ask subjects to make summaries of texts. Van Dijk and Kintsch (1983) quote studies which found that, at their first attempts at summarizing a text, subjects included a large number of elaborations and restructurings. It was only at their second attempt that details were excised to produce a short summary emphasizing the main points. These findings can be interpreted as showing that subjects were first making elaborative inferences to try to understand the text. It was only after this that they were able to make reductive inferences to identify the main topics in the macrostructure.

One important point that needs to be stressed is that each reader may end up with a different macrostructure for the same text, depending on his or her attitudes and beliefs about the topic being discussed. Two people who disagree about politics may go away with quite different macrostructures of a political speech. Years after reading a novel like *War and Peace*, the macrostructure stored in your memory may only contain the information that there are a lot of battles and a family with a charming girl called Natasha. Certainly I have a composite macrostructure for the plots of Agatha Christie stories; it is only when I start reading one of them that specific details about setting and plot remind me that I may have read this one before.

Plausible as the notions of macropropositions and macrostructures are, it is by no means easy to specify *macrorules* which determine how each particular reader will represent the gist of a story. Titles and introductions can help, but so much seems to depend on the knowledge and beliefs each reader brings to the text. Whereas you may all agree about the literal meaning of most of the sentences in this book, and even how groups of two or three sentences hang together, I wish I could feel so confident about the final macrostructure you will store in memory when you reach the last page.

This emphasis on the prior knowledge of each particular reader brings us round full circle to the issue of general knowledge versus linguistic knowledge. The analysis of larger units of language, like stories and texts, depends on general knowledge and expectations about the world. Furthermore, the macrostructures we store in memory themselves add to the knowledge we can bring to bear on the next text we read. The accumulated knowledge we gain from language results from our interpretations of everything we hear and read.

Summary of Section 5

- Discourse analysis of texts includes both local coherence and global structure.
- Local coherence is concerned with connections between sentences and involves elaborative inferences about the reference of pronouns and causal relations.
- Global structure refers to the overall gist of a passage. Van Dijk and Kintsch postulate that readers extract macropropositions to represent main themes and topics in order to build up a macrostructure for the whole text.
- Macrostructure representations stored in memory represent a person's accumulated knowledge from language sources, which in turn influences the way a language understander processes new inputs.

6   *Some conclusions*

The questions raised in Section 1 define three issues which any model of language understanding has to deal with. The first issue is how to specify the linguistic knowledge which underlies people's ability to use a particular language. This linguistic knowledge includes a lexicon of word meanings, the grammar of a language, semantic rules for combining words, and discourse rules for achieving text coherence. However, it became abundantly clear when considering these aspects of language in Sections 2 to 5 that it is simply not possible to separate purely linguistic competence from all the other types of knowledge which affect language performance. General knowledge about objects and events, goals and plans, stories and texts, all these result in inferences being made about the meanings of linguistic inputs.

A second issue raises the question of how the meanings of sentences and texts are represented. In previous sections, several different kinds of representations were described. Syntactic structure trees, representing grammatical relationships, were contrasted with case frames for expressing semantic relationships between concepts. Propositional representations of individual sentences provide the basis for extracting macropropositions to arrive at a macrostructure for a whole text.

Supporters of each approach sometimes sound as if they are describing the one and only way in which linguistic inputs are represented: syntactic structures or meanings; case frames or propositions; verbatim recall or macrostructures. But it is quite likely that any or all of these representations may be appropriate according to the circumstances. The representations we form when processing linguistic inputs are obviously very different when we try to remember the exact wording of a poem as opposed to when we are trying to understand a textbook. Representations stored in memory are likely to be different for the content of recent conversations, for quickly skimmed newspaper articles, or for books we may have read many years ago.

Finally, there is the issue of how to specify the processes involved in language understanding. All the evidence shows that different types of knowledge are used simultaneously in language understanding. Consequently, we can reject the linear stage model shown in Figure 2.1 (see page 54), replacing it with a cooperative model incorporating interactions between various types of knowledge, as shown in Figure 2.12.

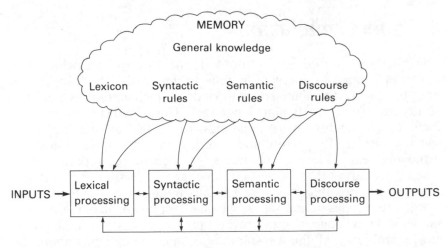

Figure 2.12   Heterarchical model of language processing

As explained earlier, the stage model in Figure 2.1 is a *hierarchical model* because each level of processing has to be completed before being passed up to the next level in the hierarchy. Unlike the one-way arrows indicating the hierarchical flow of information in Figure 2.1, the liberal profusion of two-way arrows in Figure 2.12 allows for interactions between different types of knowledge in language processing. This latter model of language understanding, known as a *heterarchical model*, consists of proces- ses which can interact with each other as required. In *heterarchical*

models control of processing passes from one component to another so that information from different types of processing can be pooled before deciding on appropriate representations for linguistic inputs.

Where models of language continue to differ is about the need for a specific component which carries out syntactic processing. Syntactically oriented models include a syntactic parser for analysing syntactic structures, even though the parser may 'consult' other components before completing the analysis. This contrasts with semantically driven models which map linguistic inputs directly on to meaningful representations. In Part III we shall be discussing some computer programs which attempt to model language understanding using various kinds of syntactic parsers and semantic analysers.

Further reading

Psychology and Language by Clark and Clark (1977) provides a comprehensive and readable account of the many processes involved in language use and language acquisition. It is full of interesting examples and summarizes the main theoretical, methodological and practical issues.

For more information about Noam Chomsky's theory and its impact on psychology you can consult *Psycholinguistics: Chomsky and Psychology* by Greene (1972) or *Thinking and Language* by Greene (1975).

There is an interesting discussion of the issues involved in the relationship between language and thought in *The Psychology of Cognition* by Cohen (1983), which includes evidence about the ability of animals to learn language and compares the cognitive development of hearing and deaf children.

Part III
Models of Language Understanding

Judith Greene

Part III   Models of Language Understanding

Contents

1   *Introduction*

At the end of Part II, I discussed those aspects of language understanding which would have to be dealt with by any model. Put at its most basic, a language model has to explain how language users are able to map linguistic inputs (sounds and letters) on to meaningful representations.

In Part I, I made the point that both linguists and cognitive psychologists are interested in the knowledge representations which underlie linguistic competence. Where psychologists differ from linguists like Chomsky is that they attempt to derive models of language from experimental investigations of the performance of language users. If subjects in an experiment confuse certain sentences, it is assumed that their mental representations of those sentences are similar. If people find it as easy to verify the truth of a passive sentence as of an active sentence, it is inferred that they are not carrying out a syntactic passive transformation but are processing the passive in its original form.

What all these experiments have in common is that language processes and representations have to be inferred from subjects' performance. It is simply not possible to ask people what processes are going on inside their heads when they read a sentence or to ask them to introspect about their representations of a sentence. If you try to introspect about how you are reading this very sentence, and how you are going to represent its meaning in your own mind, you will soon see what I mean. And I can assure you that it would be just as difficult for me to tell you what was going on inside my head while I was writing it.

The problem of investigating human language processing directly has focused interest on attempts by researchers to produce computer programs which can understand language. As we shall see, this is by no means an easy enterprise. This type of research is known as *Artificial Intelligence (AI)* because it attempts to develop computer programs which will make a computer behave 'as if' it is intelligent. Interestingly, the aim is usually stated as getting computer programs to understand *natural language*, i.e. ordinary human language with all its messy ambiguities, in contrast to the precision of the programming languages used in computer programs. AI researchers would be thrilled if they could develop a program which was able to mimic the way people manage to extract meanings from even quite simple sentences and texts.

The basic rationale for Artificial Intelligence models of language is that computers are dumb. Since computers start off with no knowledge at all about natural human languages, the researcher has to write into the program everything which is needed to make the computer behave as if it 'understands' sentences typed on the computer's keyboard. The program has to be in the form of detailed step-by-step instructions. The computer needs to be given specific information to store in its *database* 'memory' and precise programming operations for analysing inputs.

AI researchers who try to develop computer programs capable of language understanding claim that there are three major benefits:

1   The operations involved in language processing have to be stated explicitly; in other words, they have to be externalized in the form of objective instructions which a computer program can carry out. This forces the reseachers developing the program to come clean about their theory of language understanding.

2   Working out what information has to be fed into a computer's database, and what rules have to be included in the program, may reveal quite a lot about what processes must be involved in language understanding by human beings.

3   Running a program to see if it responds correctly to typed in sentences is a very good test of whether your theory of language really works.

There are, however, several problems about AI models of human language, most of which are acknowledged by AI researchers themselves. The first of these is what should count as evidence that a computer 'understands' a sentence or a text. Since computers do not go around interacting with other people in the real world, the sentences they output may simply reflect back the data the programmer has put into the program. The danger is that a program may give a false impression of understanding when all it is doing is translating one kind of linguistic representation into another.

This problem of setting criteria for evaluating the outputs of computer programs is a difficult one. Common requirements include the ability to give appropriate responses to linguistic inputs as follows:

INPUT:	OUTPUT:
Stories	Paraphrases and summaries
Questions	Answers
Instructions	Actions

But, even with these criteria, it is still difficult to decide whether a computer program 'really' understands or is just producing a limited set of preprogrammed responses. It might look impressive if you typed into a computer *What is the number of inhabitants in China?* and it typed back ONE BILLION; but it would be far less impressive if you then typed *How many eggs did I have for breakfast?* and got the same reply!

A second problem for AI programs is the vast amount of complex knowledge which seems to be required for language understanding. Apart from a vocabulary of many thousands of individual words, and syntactic and semantic rules for combining words, there is the crucial role of general knowledge. Even if computer memories were much bigger than they are, we simply do not know how to replicate the organization of human memory in a way that mirrors our ability to retrieve exactly the right knowledge to understand all the many sentences we come across, most of which we have never heard or read before in exactly that form.

For this reason, most AI language understanding programs are restricted to small *domains* of knowledge, e.g. instructions about moving toy blocks, stories about restaurants, newspaper stories describing violent events, written versions of simple arithmetic problems. Restricting the domain of a language model severely limits the vocabulary used and, even more importantly, possible senses of words. In newspaper stories about violent events the word *bank* is more likely to figure as a target for armed robbers than as a place for a peaceful fishing trip! Often the types of grammatical constructions are also limited, e.g. requests or instructions.

A final objection which is often made about AI research is that the operations used by computer programs don't necessarily tell us anything about how human minds work. Even if a program succeeds in interpreting input sentences, a human might arrive at the same interpretation in quite a different way. Nevertheless, in an area like language, where so little is understood about human abilities, it seems churlish not to acknowledge insights gained from attempts to test theories of language as working computer programs. Moreover, many AI researchers are interested in the theoretical issues which arise from attempting to model human language processing, rather than simply designing working programs. A distinction is sometimes made between Artificial Intelligence, which is concerned with getting programs to perform intelligently, and *computer simulation*, which aims to make them perform in a way that directly reflects human processing. I do not want, though, to give the impression that there is a great divide between theoretical language research and practical language understanding systems. Nearly all the models of language which will be discussed in Part III have arisen from a creative mixture of academic research and practical programming problems. And, as language is such a typically human activity, AI researchers cannot but help produce programs which simulate at least some features of human language.

Summary of Section 1

- Cognitive psychologists are interested in the knowledge representations and processes which enable language users to map linguistic inputs on to meaningful representations.
- Since people cannot introspect directly about the processes which enable them to produce and understand language, experiments have been carried out to try to elucidate the role of different kinds of knowledge and representations in language understanding.
- Another way of testing theories of language understanding is by developing Artificial Intelligence (AI) computer programs which simulate the 'intelligence' of human language users.
- Some advantages and disadvantages of AI computer programs are listed below:

Advantages	*Disadvantages*
Program instructions have to be explicit.	How do we know a program 'really' understands language?
Running a program is a good test of whether a language theory works.	Computer programs are artificially restricted to small domains of knowledge.
The information needed to make a program work may tell us a lot about human language.	Humans do not necessarily use the same processes as a computer program.

2   Early AI programs

The aim of this section is to give you an overview of the ways in which early AI language programs attempted to narrow down the language understanding problem to manageable proportions. The result is that each program represents a trade-off between good performance in the particular area the program is designed to deal with and some sort of 'fudge' to get round all the other requirements involved in language understanding. One simplification that most programs accept is that both input and output are typed words, thus bypassing the enormous problems of designing speech analysis and speech production programs which can deal with actual spoken sounds.

2.1 ELIZA

ELIZA was one of the earliest language computer programs. Its aim was to accept any kind of input from human users and to produce acceptable answers in response. As you will probably have realized by now, a program with such an ambitious aim is unlikely to be able to produce unambiguous semantic representations for all possible combinations of words.

ELIZA was developed by Weizenbaum (1966) over a period of years to simulate the language behaviour of a psychotherapist talking to a patient. It works as a dialogue system. You, playing the part of the patient, can type anything you wish into the program and get an immediate reply. The system is very 'robust'. It never breaks down into meaningless replies no matter what is said. Even if you use a word which is not in its vocabulary, it never asks for help or definitions, but continues in such a way as to cover up the fact that it has no real understanding of what has been typed in. An example of a dialogue between a human and ELIZA is given in Figure 3.1 (ELIZA's replies are in capital letters). It is instructive to compare ELIZA's dialogue with the dialogue with SAM shown in Figure 1.3 in Part I, Section 4.3.

> Men are all alike.
> IN WHAT WAY?
> They're always bugging us about something or other.
> CAN YOU THINK OF A SPECIFIC EXAMPLE?
> Well, my boyfriend made me come here.
> YOUR BOYFRIEND MADE YOU COME HERE?
> He says I'm depressed much of the time.
> I AM SORRY TO HEAR THAT YOU ARE DEPRESSED
> I need some help, that much seems certain.
> WHAT WOULD IT MEAN TO YOU IF YOU GOT SOME HELP?
> Perhaps I could learn to get along with my mother.
> TELL ME MORE ABOUT YOUR FAMILY
> My mother takes care of me.
> WHO ELSE IN YOUR FAMILY TAKES CARE OF YOU?
> My father.
> YOUR FATHER
> You are like my father in some ways.
> WHAT RESEMBLANCE DO YOU SEE?
> You don't argue with me.
> WHY DO YOU THINK I DON'T ARGUE WITH YOU?
> You are afraid of me.
> DOES IT PLEASE YOU TO THINK I AM AFRAID OF YOU?
> My father is afraid of everybody.
> WHAT ELSE COMES TO MIND WHEN YOU THINK OF YOUR FATHER?
> Bullies.
> DOES THAT HAVE ANYTHING TO DO WITH THE FACT THAT YOUR
> BOYFRIEND MADE YOU COME HERE?

Figure 3.1 Dialogue with ELIZA (adapted from Weizenbaum, 1966)

105

SAQ 33
List at least two differences between ELIZA and SAM as shown by their answers to questions in Figures 1.3 and 3.1.

The ELIZA program works by having a large store of *key words* in its database. When an input matches a key word, this is used to transform the input sentence to produce an appropriate response. For example, a 'negative' key word like *depressed* will trigger the response I AM SORRY TO HEAR THAT. . . . The word *like* makes ELIZA select the response WHAT RESEMBLANCE DO YOU SEE? The words *mother* and *father* trigger questions about your FAMILY. More subtly, the word *everybody* may elicit a response like WHO IN PARTICULAR ARE YOU THINKING OF? Other rules are responsible for turning *me* into YOU and *you* into ME so that ELIZA can reply to *You don't argue with me* with WHY DO YOU THINK I DON'T ARGUE WITH YOU?

What makes the dialogue more life-like is that the key words do not always trigger the same response. Often it depends on the context in which a key word appears. The response to the word *you* is different according to whether it occurs in the contexts *you are . . ., you . . . me* or *you are like . . .* In other words, ELIZA is capable of responding to patterns of key words as well as to single key words. Key words are also ranked so that more important words override less important words. If all else fails, the program will either choose a neutral response like TELL ME MORE or a sentence frame into which an old key word can be fitted, as in the last remark in Figure 3.1. A simple example of how ELIZA's *pattern matching* works is shown in Figure 3.2.

Humans conversing with ELIZA have sometimes been unaware that they were talking to a computer rather than a real therapist. This is partly because ELIZA mimics a 'non-directive' therapist who is expected to ask questions which reflect back the 'patient's' feelings rather than pursuing a vigorous conversation. Consequently, people are not too surprised when ELIZA asks questions about some earlier topic; for instance, since *bullies* is not one of ELIZA'S keywords, the program reverts to the BOYFRIEND topic. The truth is that ELIZA does not have a knowledge database which represents any understanding of the principles of therapy. Nor does the program incorporate a knowledge of English syntax or word meanings. A simple matching of key word patterns leads the program to select a sentence pattern into which the key words will fit. Boden (1977) gives an interesting account of ELIZA and other similar key word matching programs.

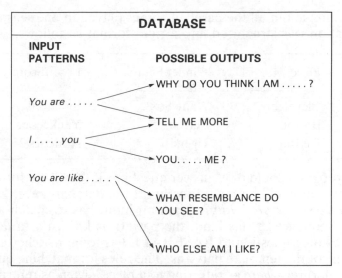

Figure 3.2   ELIZA's pattern matching

There is no doubt that Weizenbaum's ELIZA program was very successful in what it set out to do. Nevertheless, many AI researchers would not accept that such a program 'really understands' because it cannot be said to have any semantic structures that express knowledge of meanings. If it can be said to know anything, it is how to carry on a conversation without making any attempt to analyse what is being said.

Does ELIZA also violate psychological evidence about how we behave? Isn't it plausible that we sometimes engage in conversations (perhaps when bored at a party) simply by filling in slots in a pattern, as in *Do tell me more about your mother* or *That . . . certainly sounds very interesting?* In general, however, people have much greater conversational abilities than ELIZA. The program can easily be thrown if its human partner does not follow the rules of the game. For example, if you typed in *Throw the baby out with the bath water*, ELIZA might easily reply *Do you want to throw out your father too?*

2.2 *BASEBALL*

BASEBALL (Green, Wolf, Chomsky and Laughery, 1963) is an example of a question-answering program which takes exactly the opposite line to ELIZA. The database of BASEBALL contained information about all the baseball games played in one season. This information was structured into a rigid format as follows:

Month	Place	Day	Winner/Score	Loser/Score
July	Cleveland	6	White Sox/2	Indians/0
July	Boston	7	Red Sox/5	Yankees/3
July	Detroit	7	Tigers/10	Athletics/2

The program could only answer questions if they were formulated in a way that could be read directly off the database, e.g. *Who did the Yankees play on 7 July?* When an input has to match a whole pattern sequence of this kind, the pattern is known as a *template*. Any incoming question to BASEBALL has to be matched to see if it fits one of the template patterns. The rules for matching questions would interpret *where* as referring to a place, *when* as referring to a date, and so on.

SAQ 34
Based on the information in the database given above, write down the replies BASEBALL would give to:
(a) *Where did the White Sox play the Indians?*
(b) *What were the scores of the winners and losers of all games played on 7 July?*
(c) *Which team played the White Sox in Boston?*

The disadvantage of BASEBALL is that a question like *What do you think of baseball?* would receive the reply I DO NOT UNDERSTAND. The disadvantage with ELIZA is that, given a statement like *My father is a giraffe*, the program would respond with TELL ME MORE ABOUT YOUR FAMILY. BASEBALL'S understanding is complete but totally restricted; ELIZA's understanding is nil but allows the possibility of plausible remarks on any topic. As you will see in later sections, this tension between knowledge and flexibility exists in all AI language understanding programs.

Summary of Section 2

- ELIZA and BASEBALL were two early AI language understanding programs. ELIZA was designed to simulate the responses of a non-directive therapist. BASEBALL was designed to provide information about baseball games.
- ELIZA and BASEBALL can be compared under the following headings:

	ELIZA	BASEBALL
DOMAIN	Any topic	Baseball games
INPUT	'Patient's' remarks	Questions
OUTPUT	'Therapist's' comments and questions	Answers
KNOWLEDGE	Key word patterns	Template format for games information
PROCESSES	Matches inputs against key word patterns	Matches questions against templates
ADVANTAGES	Makes plausible responses to a wide range of remarks	Provides comprehensive information about a set of baseball games
DISADVANTAGES	No semantic under-understanding of 'therapy' domain; sometimes asks silly questions	Can only be interrogated in a set format about games stored in its database

3   *Winograd's SHRDLU*

Winograd's account of a language understanding program called SHRDLU caused a tremendous stir in 1972 and had an important influence on later generations of AI programs. SHRDLU was the antithesis of ELIZA in that it attempted to represent real understanding of a small domain. The program was the antithesis of BASEBALL because knowledge was represented in a flexible way rather than as a stereotyped format.

Before Winograd's (1972) work, AI programs which were able to deal with a topic in depth tended to be rather bad at English. For example, there were programs which could respond to typed commands to solve algebra problems; but the English they accepted was very stylized. They knew quite a lot about algebra, but you had to type in fixed patterns such as *What is the value of x now?* You could not vary any of these words if the program was to understand you. Such a program has none of our human ability to analyse the meanings of sentences in order to see that quite different sentences like *Can you help me?* and *Give me a hand* are 'saying the same thing'.

3.1   The blocks world

Although Winograd's program aimed to give a very general analysis of the process involved in language understanding, it was limited to a very small domain. This was an imaginary world of toy blocks: pyramids and boxes which can be moved about by a 'crane'. A picture of the blocks appeared on the computer's video screen (see Figure 3.3).

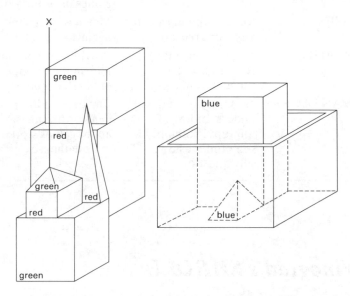

Figure 3.3   SHRDLU: Blocks world (adapted from Winograd, 1972)

If the program understood a command typed into the computer, it 'executed' the instructions by 'moving' blocks which caused the video picture to change. The program could also answer questions about what it intended to do and make statements about what it had done. A sample dialogue with SHRDLU is given in Figure 3.4 (as usual, the computer's output is in capital letters). I expect you will be pretty impressed by SHRDLU'S responses, especially its answer to the question *Does the shortest thing the tallest pyramid's support supports support anything green?* You may like to check SHRDLU'S accuracy against the situation shown in Figure 3.3. The basis for SHRDLU'S abilities will be explained in the next section.

SAQ 35
Look back to Figure 1.3 in Part I, Figure 3.1 in Section 2 of this part, and Figure 3.4. Are the responses given by SHRDLU more like SAM'S or more like ELIZA'S?

What does the box contain?
THE BLUE PYRAMID AND THE BLUE BLOCK
What is the pyramid supported by?
THE BOX
How many blocks are not in the box?
SIX OF THEM
Can the table pick up blocks?
NO
Can a pyramid support a pyramid?
I DON'T KNOW
Does the shortest thing the tallest pyramid's support supports support anything green?
YES, THE GREEN PYRAMID
Will you please stack up both of the red blocks and either a green cube or a pyramid?
OK
Had you touched any pyramid before you put the green one on the little cube?
YES, THE GREEN ONE
When did you pick it up?
WHILE I WAS STACKING UP THE RED CUBE, A LARGE RED BLOCK AND A LARGE
GREEN CUBE

Figure 3.4 Dialogue with SHRDLU (adapted from Winograd, 1972)

3.2 Three modules

One of the key features of SHRDLU is that the program has
separate *modules* which know about different features of natural
language and the blocks world. Figure 3.5 shows the three modules
incorporated in the SHRDLU program. The Syntax module
contains syntactic rules, the Semantics module contains a lexicon
and semantic rules for building up semantic representations, and the
Blocks module contains general knowledge – limited, of course, to
the world of toy blocks.

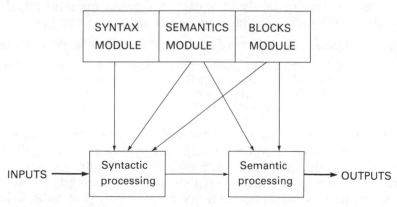

Figure 3.5   SHRDLU modules

Winograd argued that these modules must be able to pass information to each other when needed. Rather than a strict hierarchy in which information is always passed in a fixed order, the modules should be organized as a *heterarchy* in which control can be passed from one component to another as required. You can see the need to consult different modules by considering the command, *Put the green pyramid on the block in the box*. In terms of a syntactic analysis, there are two possible ways to group the noun phrases in the sentence:

1 *Put (the green pyramid) on (the block in the box)*, i.e. move the green pyramid and place it on top of a block which is already in the box.
2 *Put (the green pyramid on the block) in (the box)*, i.e. move the green pyramid, which is now on top of a block, and put it on the floor of the box.

SAQ 36
Using brackets, as in the above example, write down two possible syntactic analyses for the sentence *John went down the road in a bus*. Why is one interpretation unlikely to be taken seriously?

To deal with a potentially ambiguous sentence like *Put the green pyramid on the block in the box*, the Syntax module in Winograd's program is able to call on the Semantics module and the Blocks module to settle which of the two possible syntactic analyses is correct. For instance, the Semantics module would confirm that the verb *put* and each of the blocks referred to make sense. At this point, reference would be made to the Blocks module. Referring to its knowledge of where all the blocks are (as shown in Figure 3.3), it would report that either interpretation is possible because the green pyramid is at present on a red block and so could be moved from there to the floor of the box; equally the green pyramid could be placed on top of the blue block which is already in the box.

SAQ 37
Look at Figure 3.6. Which of the two possible syntactic interpretations of *Put the green pyramid on the block in the box* (see (1) and (2) above) would be accepted by the Blocks module for the state of the blocks world shown in (a) of Figure 3.6? And which interpretation would it accept for the state of blocks in (b)?

We will now consider how each of the modules operates in more detail. The Syntax module contains parsing rules which identify syntactic constituents of sentences like noun phrases and verb phrases. These rules are very like the Augmented Transition Networks (ATNs) described in Section 3.4 of Part II. The basic idea is that the program works through a sentence, taking each word in

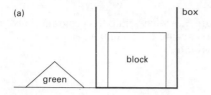 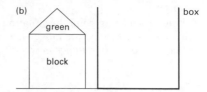

Figure 3.6

turn, in order to build up a network which identifies each group of words as a noun phrase (NP), verb (V), and so on. The syntactic rules would start by analysing the first words of a sentence; for instance, *put* would be identified as the imperative form of a verb because it starts a sentence. This in turn would trigger a search for an NP, the conditions for which would be met by *the green pyramid*.

At this point in the sentence, the verb *put* and the NP *the green pyramid* would be passed over to the Semantics module to see if this phrase makes sense. The Semantics module contains word definitions and also rules for combining words to compile meaningful representations of possible actions. For instance, the meaning of a verb like *put* would be represented as meaning the actual actions involved in moving a block and placing it somewhere else. *The green pyramid* would be interpreted as an object which (a) is a block; (b) has a pyramid shape; (c) has a green colour; and so is identified as a possible object in the blocks world. The Semantics module contains information about objects and events which are possible in general (even though they may not be possible in a particular state of the blocks world). For instance, it is the knowledge in the Semantics module which prompted SHRDLU to say that it is impossible for a table to pick up a block (see Figure 3.4). However, since the fact that pyramids cannot support other pyramids is not represented in the Semantics module, SHRDLU replied I DON'T KNOW to that question. It is possible for the program to be asked to try stacking two pyramids, one on top of the other, and, in the event of failure, to log this new bit of information in the Semantics module.

Once a sentence has been interpreted as making sense, it has to be tested out in the 'real' world, making use of knowledge in the Blocks module. It was one of the most novel features of Winograd's system that interpretations could be checked against the current position of the blocks to see whether they refer to possible moves. This enabled SHRDLU to make inferences about possible interpretations based on general knowledge about the world. As you will have noticed in the sample dialogue in Figure 3.4, SHRDLU can carry out complicated manoeuvres to move blocks around and can also give a verbal report of its reasons for doing so.

SAQ 38
Taking as a starting point the situation in Figure 3.3, what would the program reply
if it were asked to list the moves necessary to execute the command *Put the small
red cube into the box under the small blue pyramid?*

3.3   Evaluation of SHRDLU

What is so impressive about SHRDLU is that the program was able
to make inferences based on both linguistic knowledge and real-life
knowledge in order to interpret commands. The program could also
work out what moves were necessary to execute a command and to
give a reasoned account of its actions. Another characteristic of
SHRDLU is that its meaning representations were formulated as
procedures for carrying out actions, a type of semantics which is
often called *procedural semantics*. This was partly a function of
SHRDLU's activities in the blocks world. However, there has been
support for the notion that at least some of our knowledge,
especially highly learned skills, is stored and run off as preprogrammed procedures. For instance, skills like driving a car or tying a
shoelace are examples of *procedural knowledge*. This is contrasted
with *declarative knowledge* which represents facts that we know.
Procedural knowledge and declarative knowledge are sometimes
contrasted as 'knowing how' to do something, e.g. run a mile, as
opposed to 'knowing that' – or at least believing that – such and
such is a fact, e.g. jogging is good for you.

But perhaps the most important point about Winograd's program
is that its interpretations of commands and questions were based on
a real understanding of what was going on in the blocks world. The
crucial difference between SHRDLU and its predecessors, like
ELIZA and BASEBALL, is that SHRDLU could make inferences
based on its knowledge of what was possible in its world. Both
ELIZA and BASEBALL operated by matching the surface
structures of sentences against patterns stored in their databases.
SHRDLU used linguistic and general knowledge to compile
meaningful representations of inputs. This gave the program much
greater flexibility in interpreting and generating appropriate
responses and, of course, makes it a far more plausible model of
human language processes.

Undoubtedly, Winograd's program was a great step forward, and
many features of SHRDLU have influenced the development of AI
natural language programs. In particular, SHRDLU emphasized
the need for interaction between the Syntax, Semantics and Blocks
modules. You should notice, however, that the SHRDLU model of
language understanding is still a *modular system* in the sense of

having separate modules to represent different kinds of knowledge. It comes into the category of models which have a separate syntactic parser (the Syntax module), the output of which is not unlike Chomsky's syntactic structure trees representing the relationships between NPs, VPs and other syntactic categories. Moreover, it is the Syntax module which calls in the Semantics and Blocks modules to check the accuracy of its syntactic analysis. In this sense Winograd's system is a heterarchical model which is syntactically driven. It is only when a sentence has been parsed that it is compiled as a procedure for action.

Summary of Section 3

- Winograd's computer program SHRDLU was a great step forward in modelling the human language understander's ability to produce meaningful representations using knowledge-based inferences.
- SHRDLU included three modules, Syntax, Semantics and Blocks, organized as a heterarchical system in which the modules can be called in to aid the analysis of inputs.
- Some of the characteristics of SHRDLU are listed below:

DOMAIN	World of toy blocks
INPUT	Commands and questions
OUTPUT	Actions and answers
MODULES:	
Syntax	Parsing rules
Semantics	Lexicon and semantic rules
Blocks (world knowledge)	Information about state of blocks world
PROCESSES	Compiles procedural representations by a mixture of syntactic parsing, semantic interpretation and checking state of blocks
ADVANTAGES	'Knows' what it is talking about; ability to make inferences on the basis of linguistic and general knowledge
DISADVANTAGES	Understanding is limited to a small number of objects and events in a toy blocks world; only needs to resolve the few ambiguities possible in that world.

4   Schank's model of language understanding

Roger Schank and his Artificial Intelligence group at Yale University have been working on language understanding for many years during which their ideas have developed in several directions. Some of these have been mentioned in earlier sections and I will now attempt to bring them together.

In Section 4.3 of Part I, Schank's theory of *scripts* was introduced. These are schemas which represent knowledge about routine actions occurring in various situations, such as visiting restaurants or doctors. The computer program SAM used scripts to make sense of script-based stories by making inferences about probable sequences of events.

In Section 2.4 of Part II, Schank's list of *semantic primitives* was introduced as a method for analysing the meanings of verbs in terms of a few basic Acts, e.g. ATRANS (transfer of possession), MTRANS (transfer of mental information), PROPEL (applying force), and INGEST. These primitives were defined by case frames specifying what kinds of entities would make suitable Actors, Objects and Recipients for each verb.

As described in Sections 4.1 and 4.2 of Part II, Schank's model postulates a semantic analyser for extracting sentence representations, as opposed to models which require a separate stage of syntactic parsing. The basic idea is that sentences can be mapped directly on to case frames which represent semantic relationships between the concepts described by words and sentences. Figure 2.11 gives some examples of Schank's Conceptual Dependency networks (which can also be expressed in a case frame format) for sentences.

So how do all these bits and pieces fit together into one coherent model? The following sections will show how Schank's research group developed a series of computer programs to tackle some of the multifarious problems of modelling human language understanding (Schank, 1980).

4.1   Conceptual Dependencies revisited: MARGIE

The aim of Conceptual Dependency (CD) representations, as described in Part II, Section 4.2, is to represent the meanings of sentences in such a way that inferences can be made about possible interpretations. An important point about CD representations is that they themselves are non-linguistic. By this I mean that they represent our mental concepts about the structure of real-life events. For instance, the CD representation of *Mary bought the book from John* is intended to encapsulate all the inferences we might make about a real-life episode involving the purchase of books. Inferences might include that there is a transfer of possession (ATRANS) of money and a book, that Mary wants the book, either to read or to sell again, that John needs money, that John may be a bookseller.

Schank argues that inferences like these are necessary to understand possible follow-up sentences like *John was able to pay off his Access bill* or *Mary wanted to read 'War and Peace'*. An immediate problem, though, is that in principle there is no limit to the number of inferences that might follow from any one situation. *Mary was able to get down to her A-level revision* is easy to understand if we make the 'bridging' inference that the book was an A-level text book. But what about *How odd, I thought Mary couldn't read, John was lucky to get rid of it, Was it by mail order?*, or *She needed a door stop?* All these sentences need to be interpreted on the basis of inferences implied by the CD for *Mary bought the book from John*: e.g. that books are for reading, that people who sell things no longer possess them, that sales can be carried out in many ways and that the object of ATRANS might be a physical object which can be used to hold a door open. This potential proliferation of possible inferences is sometimes known as the *inferential explosion*.

SAQ 39
(a) List as many inferences as you can think of which might follow from *John punched Bill*.
(b) Suggest some follow-up sentences which might be interpreted on the basis of these inferences.

It was easy enough to demonstrate in Part I that humans make bridging inferences which 'go beyond' the literal meanings of sentences in order to interpret utterances and texts. But this is where AI computer models come into their own. In order to get a program to interpret sentences, Schank had to specify exactly what knowledge needs to be input into the computer's database and the exact sequence of operations to be carried out by the program in order to make any necessary inferences.

One early attempt at building a language understanding computer system was called MARGIE. MARGIE stands for the long-winded title Memory Analysis Response Generation and Inference on English. The program included a semantic *Analyser* for 'parsing' sentences into Conceptual Dependencies (CDs) which has access to a Lexicon, and an *Inferencer* program for drawing appropriate inferences (see Figure 3.7). In relation to Winograd's SHRDLU modules shown in Figure 3.5, the Analyser performs the functions of both the Syntax and Semantic modules. The Inferencer is analogous to the Blocks module because it makes inferences about the real-life situations represented by CDs.

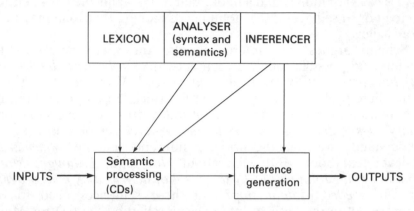

Figure 3.7   MARGIE modules

MARGIE's first step is for the Analyser to analyse input sentences into CD case frame representations. The Analyser works by selecting a semantic primitive Act for each verb and filling in case slots with any appropriate Actors, Objects, and Recipients mentioned in the sentence. The Analyser refers to a lexicon of case frames for each Act, specifying the types of entities that can occur in the slots.

Given the sentence *John gave Mary the book*, the Analyser selects ATRANS as the most likely Act to represent the verb *give*. The program then tests whether expectations set up by a particular Act are present in the sentence. When it comes to *John* it assigns *John* to the Actor slot. The next word *Mary* is rejected for the Object slot because the object of *give* has to be non-human, i.e. an object or possibly a pet animal; so *Mary* is assigned as a possible Recipient (represented by Direction TO). Since the only remaining word *book* is a suitable object, it is allocated to the Object slot. The final CD representation for the sentence would be:

> Actor: *John*
> Act: ATRANS
> Object: *book*
> Direction TO: *Mary*
>   FROM: *John*

With a passive sentence like *John was given a book by Mary*, the Analyser would again start by allocating *John* to the Actor slot. But when it comes to the passive verb followed by the word *by*, this 'passive' indicator triggers off a reorganization of slots, putting *Mary* in the Actor slot and *John* in the Direction TO slot.

SAQ 40
Draw a CD representation using (a) a case frame format and (b) a network format for the sentence *John punched Bill*. HINT:Look back to Sections 4.1 and 4.2 of Part II and Figure 2.11.

MARGIE's next step is to call in the Inferencer program to add inferences which follow from the situation represented in the CD. These are based on several different types of inferences about actions and states. The most important are inferences about what might have caused the situation and what might result from the action. These can be used to build up *causal chains* of probable events. An example of some inferences which MARGIE might have made about *John punched Bill* are shown in Figure 3.8 overleaf.

I expect you have realized that the causal chain of actions and states shown in Figure 3.8 is only one of many possible scenarios that could be inferred from the original sentence *John punched Bill*. In fact, one major problem with the MARGIE program was that it had no idea which inferences might be relevant and so was committed to generating all potential causes and results of each situation. The only thing which checked the inferential explosion was the practical limit of knowledge in MARGIE's database about likely causes and consequences of events. For instance, if MARGIE knows nothing about boxing, she will not make the appropriate inference to make sense of *John punched Bill. The referee declared John the champion.*

Because Schank wanted to develop a computer system to understand whole stories, he went on to design programs which built in restrictions on MARGIE's propensity for generating inferences. However, there are two characteristics of MARGIE which have remained important in Schank's model of language understanding:

1 Sentences should be analysed by semantically driven parsers which operate by testing for possible words to fill the slots in conceptual case frames.
2 Sentences should be mapped on to CD representations of non-linguistic situations on the basis of which inferences can be made to produce causal chains of CDs.

119

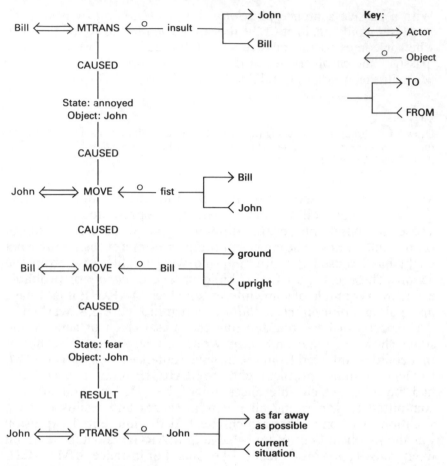

Figure 3.8

4.2   Scripts revisited: SAM

This, at long last, is where scripts come in. When Schank's group attempted to write computer programs to interpret stories rather than single sentences, they had to find a method for picking out a connected set of inferences from all the numerous inferences generated by MARGIE. The whole point about scripts is that they organize inferences into causal chains of CDs which represent sequences of events in a script situation. Once a story is recognized as referring to a restaurant, the program confines itself to churning out inferences relevant to restaurant scripts. To demonstrate the critical role of scripts as inference organizers, Figure 3.9 shows the Restaurant script as a list of causally connected CD representations.

script:	Restaurant
roles:	customer, waitress, chef, cashier
reason:	to get food so as to go up in pleasure and down in hunger
scene 1:	*Entering*
	PTRANS self into restaurant
	ATTEND eyes to where empty tables are
	MBUILD where to sit
	PTRANS self to table
	MOVE sit down
scene 2:	*Ordering*
	ATRANS menu from waitress
	MTRANS menu
	MBUILD what self wants
	MTRANS order to waitress
scene 3:	*Eating*
	ATRANS receive food from waitress
	INGEST food
scene 4:	*Exiting*
	MTRANS ask for bill
	ATRANS bill from waitress
	ATRANS tip to waitress
	PTRANS self to cashier
	ATRANS money to cashier
	PTRANS self out of restaurant

Figure 3.9 Restaurant script (adapted from Schank and Abelson, 1977a)

You should turn back to Figure 1.2 in Part I to make sure you understand why the two versions of the Restaurant script are identical. It is simply that the actions in Figure 1.2 are written in English whereas in Figure 3.9 they are shown as CD representations. You should note that even in Figure 3.9 the Acts are shorthand for full CDs. For instance, PTRANS *self into restaurant* would be represented by the following case frame:

Actor: *Customer*

Act: PTRANS

Object: *Customer*

Direction TO: *inside restaurant*

FROM: *outside restaurant*

SAQ 41
(a) Which actions in Figure 1.2 have been left out of the CDs in Figure 3.9?
(b) Draw a CD (in network format) for MBUILD *where to sit*.

If you look back to the sample of SAM dialogue in Figure 1.3, perhaps you can now understand more clearly where all the inferences come from that are stated in the paraphrase. In the course of understanding the *John ate lobster* story, SAM works out all the causal chains for the facts stated in the story, e.g. that John must have read the menu before he can order. SAM can also answer questions about the reasons for actions. By inferring that John needs to be given a menu before he can order, SAM can give the answer SO HE COULD ORDER in reply to the question *Why did John get a menu?*.

Let us now consider in more detail how SAM manages to analyse input sentences and to make appropriate inferences in order to generate responses. The whole SAM system consists of a suite of computer programs, including a semantic analyser for mapping inputs on to CD representations, known as ELI (English Language Interpreter). There is also *PP Memory* (Picture Producer Memory) which operates as a lexicon of word meanings. Finally, at the heart of the system, is SAM itself (*Script Applier Mechanism*), the program which makes inferences about script actions. As in Winograd's SHRDLU, these program modules can call on each other when necessary (see Figure 3.10).

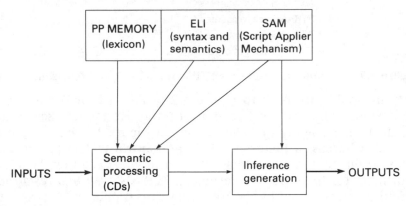

Figure 3.10   SAM modules

Like the Analyser in MARGIE, ELI works by looking for words which fit the requirements for case frame slots. The output of this analysis is a CD for each sentence. The lexicon in PP Memory searches the CD representations to see whether there are any names it recognizes (e.g. names of restaurants) and adds information about other word meanings: for instance, that a *sausage* is edible, and that *chairs, sofas* and *benches* are all for sitting on but that some are more likely to be found in one situation than another.

If there is no obvious script identifier, SAM comes into operation to try to match sequences of CDs against the causal chains of CDs in the scripts it knows about. For example, MOVE *sit down* followed by ATRANS *menu from waitress* is likely to occur in a Restaurant script, MOVE *sit down* followed by PTRANS *to doctor's office* is likely to be part of a Visiting the doctor script, MOVE *sit down* followed by MTRANS *from professor* would trigger a Lecture script.

Once a particular script has been activated, all the modules in the whole SAM system go into overdrive. The ELI analyser uses the information about probable causal chains to guide its choice of CD representations for future sentences; PP Memory attributes names and word meanings which are suitable for the currently activated script; and SAM makes inferences about actions which are likely to occur next.

Let us take as an example the sentence *John entered McDonalds*. ELI would analyse this into the following Conceptual Dependency (CD) frame:

Actor: *John*

Act: PTRANS

Object: *John*

Direction TO: *McDonalds*

FROM: somewhere outside McDonalds

PP Memory would identify *McDonalds* as the name of a particular restaurant. SAM would use the name of the restaurant to activate the Restaurant script and would find a match between the CD and the first event in the script: PTRANS *self into restaurant*. SAM would then notify PP Memory that the name *John* is a good candidate for the 'customer' role. When the next sentence is input, all the component programs of SAM are set to expect more information that is relevant to the Restaurant script. If the next sentence is *John gave a tip*, this would be interpreted as ATRANS *money to waitress* (rather than as MTRANS *advice about horses*, an interpretation which would be more likely in a Racing script).

However, several difficulties emerged in the implementation of SAM as a language understanding system. The first of these is the problem of how to handle deviations from a script, such as an unexpected event. Schank and Abelson (1977a) talk about storing some actions on a 'weird list'. But this raises the more general issue of how to represent the actual events in a story when they conflict with expected default values for script events, e.g. John chatting up the waitress instead of ordering. The crux of the problem is that a

'Flirting' script is being infiltrated into the Restaurant script. Keeping track of all the scripts which may be relevant to stories describing real-life events is no mean feat.

This raises the even more problematic issue of script selection. Identification of scripts is crucial to SAM's success, yet it is often the case that the opening sentences of stories could refer to several different possible scripts. Some 40 to 50 scripts were written for SAM, although typically only a few scripts were fed into the computer at any one time. For instance, when dealing with newspaper stories, SAM usually had only a few likely scripts to select from (e.g. disasters, conferences). Despite this limitation, selection of appropriate scripts is one of the trickiest problems for SAM. *John went to a restaurant and ate lobster* may pose no problems. But it is much more common to find that scripts are embedded in each other or implied by other scripts. The sentence *John decided to go to a museum* activates the Museum script, but SAM also needs to know that a trip to a museum may involve Subway or Bus scripts and, while in the museum, Restaurant, Ticket, Cloakroom and many other scripts.

The use of scripts to confine inferences to those relevant to an activated script certainly helps to curb the inferential explosion. But, even within a single script, there are still a very large number of inferences which can be made. For instance, ATRANS *menu from waitress* implies that the customer probably signalled to the waitress, that she walked over to the table by putting one foot in front of the other, holding the menu in her hand, and placed it either on the table or in the customer's hand. These inferences may be necessary to understand a sentence like *When she walked over to the table she realized she had left the menu on the counter*, implying a certain degree of absent-mindedness which might set off a whole new chain of inferences.

In principle, it would be possible to write all these inferences into the SAM program. However, one drawback of programs which make a lot of inferences, like MARGIE and SAM, and SHRDLU for that matter, is that they use up a lot of computer time to analyse even the simplest sentence. When you consider that a computer can carry out millions of calculations in a fraction of a second, any program that takes several minutes to interpret the meaning of *John went to a restaurant and ate lobster* can't be using the same language understanding processes as humans.

4.3   Sketchy scripts: FRUMP

One approach to this problem was the development of a script-based program known as FRUMP (Fast Reading Understanding and Memory Program). Riesbeck (1985) describes FRUMP as an example of a *Realistic Language Comprehension (RLC)* system. By this he means a language understanding program which can deal with ordinary texts like newspaper stories in less than a minute, as opposed to programs which take many minutes to understand even specially selected sentences like *John gave the book to Mary*.

FRUMP (De Jong, 1982) works by applying world knowledge in its analysis of newspaper items. The knowledge in FRUMP's database is organized in a script-like fashion but takes the form of *sketchy scripts*. They are called sketchy because they list only the most important events rather than all the detailed actions involved. An English rendering of the order of events in a Demonstration sketchy script is shown in Figure 3.11. Script events are actually formalized as causal chains of Conceptual Dependencies in the FRUMP program.

Predicted Event 1:
    The demonstrators arrive at the demonstration location.
Predicted Event 2:
    The demonstrators march.
Predicted Event 3:
    Police arrive on the scene.
Predicted Event 4:
    The demonstrators communicate with the target of the demonstration.
Predicted Event 5:
    The demonstrators attack the target of the demonstration.
Predicted Event 6:
    The demonstrators attack the police.
Predicted Event 7:
    The police attack the demonstrators.
Predicted Event 8:
    The police arrest the demonstrators.

Figure 3.11   Demonstration sketchy script (adapted from De Jong, 1982)

SAQ 42
Write down a CD (case frame format) to represent Predicted Event 1 in the Demonstration sketchy script in Figure 3.11.

The module which contains sketchy scripts predicts likely sequences of events, and so is called the *Predictor* module of FRUMP. There is a second module called the *Substantiator* and there is also a lexicon of word definitions (see Figure 3.12). As De Jong points out, compared with the SAM system, the Predictor can loosely be equated with the Script Applier Mechanism (SAM) and the Substantiator with the semantic analyser (ELI). The crucial difference between FRUMP and SAM lies in the relation between the two modules in each system. As you can see in Figure 3.10, in SAM processing starts with ELI producing sentence representations (CDs) on which the Script Applier Mechanism can get to work. While there is interaction between the modules, the final representation of the text is built-up from an appropriate selection of CD representations.

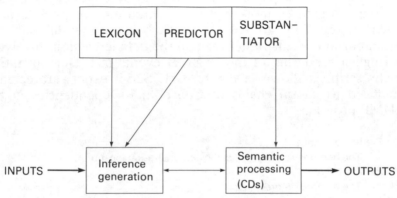

Figure 3.12   FRUMP modules

In FRUMP the roles of the two modules are completely reversed. At the very beginning of a story, it is true, the first few words have to be analysed by the Substantiator. But, from that point on, the Predictor is in control. It hazards a guess about which sketchy scripts are relevant and asks the Substantiator to search the text to see if these are confirmed. The analyser module is called the Substantiator because its only purpose is to substantiate, i.e. test out the hypotheses of the Predictor. The two-way relationship between the predictions made by the Predictor and the evidence found by the Substantiator is shown by the two-way arrow between inference generation and semantic processing in Figure 3.12.

An important consequence of this arrangement is that analysis into CD representations is only carried out on those sentences which the Predictor thinks are relevant. Let us take as an example the following short newspaper story:

> *The demonstrators charged the police. The blonde girl was making a pot. A policeman fired above their heads and the girl was arrested.*

Having decided that this story can be interpreted by the Demonstration sketchy script, the Predictor would only be looking for predicted events. So, when the Substantiator goes through the text it would not produce an analysis of the sentence about the blonde girl, nor would it be foxed by the possible meaning of *fired* as in firing a pot. In interpreting newspaper stories there is a constant interaction between the Predictor and the Substantiator. But it is the fact that the program operates under the control of the Predictor which made FRUMP so relatively fast. As Riesbeck (1985) says, 'Once FRUMP had a script, it never asked "which meaning of this word is right"? Instead it asked "Can this word mean what I want it to?"'.

Sometimes FRUMP's singlemindedness leads it to find support for its predictions even where none exists. One example is the way FRUMP interpreted the headline *Pope's Death Shakes the Western Hemisphere* as THERE WAS AN EARTHQUAKE IN THE WESTERN HEMISPHERE. THE POPE DIED. The fact that FRUMP interpreted the word *shakes* as fulfilling the predicted *land moves* event in the Earthquake sketchy script demonstrates one of FRUMP's weaknesses: its tendency to ignore anything it is not interested in. Moreover, like all script-based programs, FRUMP can only interpret sequences of actions that fit in with its prestored scripts. For instance, you may have noticed in Figure 3.11 that, according to FRUMP, Predicted Event 6 is always supposed to precede Predicted Event 7, which might make it difficult for FRUMP to deal with stories in which these two events are reversed.

On the other hand, FRUMP's refusal to consider any other possible meanings of potentially ambiguous phrases cuts out the long processing times which other analysers need in order to generate a lot of detailed inferences in order to select one interpretation rather than another. This means that FRUMP can analyse real newspaper stories quite rapidly. You should note, though, that these stories were in fact the short items produced by newspaper agencies, like Reuters or the American UPI, which concentrate on the main news items without including any of the extra details which might baffle FRUMP.

In one test FRUMP was run with seven of its sketchy scripts active simultaneously, including 'Meetings', 'Accusations', 'War', 'Agreements', 'Making' and 'Breaking' diplomatic relations, and 'Giving aid'. Out of 120 stories, FRUMP gave correct or nearly correct interpretations of 67 stories and failed to give an interpretation and/or misinterpreted the remaining stories. This may not sound all that good, but it is in fact a very successful performance for a language understanding program faced with genuine news items.

4.4   Beyond scripts: MOPS

One problem with both SAM and FRUMP is that they are limited to certain prestored script situations, whether these are expressed as a detailed list of all actions involved (SAM) or as a sketchy list of the main events (FRUMP). Unlike these programs, human users find it easy to understand stories which involve deviations from scripts and an interplay among several scripts. Schank was also particularly struck by the findings from the experiment by Bower, Black and Turner (1979) described in Techniques Box D in Part I. This was the experiment which showed that people tend to muddle up actions from similar scripts, such as events in waiting rooms.

This led Schank (1985) to suggest that people's knowledge is not stored in the form of preset sequences of actions. Rather we are able to draw on all kinds of knowledge in order to create representations which will help us understand a particular situation. Instead of being prestored as a single script, our knowledge of likely script events can be brought together to create a script-like representation whenever this is required on each particular occasion.

Schank has developed this notion of creating scripts on demand as part of a general theory of *dynamic memory* (Schank, 1982b). The basic idea is that memories are organized at many different levels. Instead of a rigid distinction between *semantic memory*, incorporating general knowledge, and *episodic memory*, incorporating specific personal experiences, Schank suggests that memories are stored at many levels ranging from the most specific to the most general.

When we read a story about going to MacDonalds, this may stimulate memories (i.e. remind us) about the last time we went to that particular MacDonalds or to a fast-food restaurant of any kind, or about characteristics of restaurants in general. If we think the bill is exorbitant, or that the waitress is pretty, memories relating to non-payment of bills or flirting may be called in although they are not part of the restaurant script. According to Schank, the only part of the old Restaurant script which would still be stored as a sequence of routine actions would be actions that are specific to restaurants, e.g. summoning waitresses and reading menus. All the other events would be part of more general memory representations about entering buildings, tipping, paying bills and eating.

SAQ 43
Look back to Figure 1.4 in Part I. Which of the actions in the 'Visiting doctor' script would be included in a specific Doctor script and which would be stored as more general memory representations?

As usual, Schank gives these general memory representations a catchy name, *MOPs*, which stands for *Memory Organization Packets*. They are given this name because they represent collections (packets) of knowledge organized around a central theme. MOPs are derived from similar experiences, such as 'waiting rooms', 'paying bills', 'contracting professional services', and what doctors and dentists do. In order to interpret a particular visit to a restaurant or a doctor, relevant MOPs would be recalled in order to construct a *superscript* for that particular occasion. As you may have realized, Memory Organization Packets (MOPS) are just a new name for *schemas*, which were defined in Part I as encapsulating our knowledge about everything connected with a particular object or event.

One problem with scripts was that actions, such as entering buildings, asking for services and making appointments, had to be separately listed in each script. It is a great advantage of MOPs that they cut out the wastefulness of storing information about, say, paying bills, under each and every script that involves paying for services. Under the new system, paying bills would be stored as a separate MOP which can be used to reconstruct many different superscripts. The 'old' scripts used in SAM would now be much smaller since all the general actions common to many scripts would be extracted as MOPs for storage elsewhere.

So how do MOPs work in practice? Imagine that you are reading a story about a visit to a doctor. Instead of referring to a routine sequence of actions in a Doctor script, all possible MOPs will be waiting in the wings to be brought in as required depending on the way the story turns out. If nothing special happens in the waiting room, none of the MOPs relevant to waiting room events will be activated. But if the character in the story sees a large white rabbit sitting behind the doctor's desk, all kinds of bizarre MOPs may come to mind. These will include a MOP representing the normal range of events expected in a doctor's office, plus other MOPs to try to explain the deviation: e.g. a 'psychiatric patient' MOP, a 'fantasy story' MOP, and so on. Instead of trying to follow just one rigid path through a prescribed sequence of actions, the many potential combinations of MOPs allow for interpretations of each occasion as a special event. Figure 3.13 overleaf shows some MOPs which might be relevant to understanding a story about calling in a plumber to fix an overflowing drain.

SAQ 44
Which MOPS in Figure 3.13 would need to be changed to account for a visit to a lawyer?

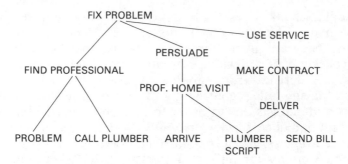

Figure 3.13   Plumber MOPs (adapted from Schank, 1985)

One problem with MOPs, as with all schema representations of knowledge, is that, when we generalize our knowledge of many visits to restaurants, to professionals, etc., we begin to forget the specific details of each visit. Schank argues that this is a small price to pay for the advantages of memories being organized so that they can cope with many situations. In fact, he points out that it is just because we are 'reminded' of other similar events through common MOPs that we are able to interpret novel situations. For instance, if we saw a demonstration in which there was an unexpected sequence of events, we – unlike FRUMP – would be able to blend together relevant MOPs based on previous experiences in order to construct a superscript to account for the new situation.

4.5   Using MOPS in IPP

Schank and his colleagues (Schank, Lebowitz and Birnbaum, 1978) developed a set of programs called *IPP* (Integrated Partial Parsing). Basically IPP operates in the same way as FRUMP in that it searches through a text looking for events which confirm its predictions. But, instead of including script sequences of actions, however sketchy, the knowledge in IPP's database is stored in the form of MOPs. Because it can refer to several MOPs at once, IPP is less likely to go overboard by selecting just one sketchy script and ignoring all other information. The organization of the modules in IPP is shown in Figure 3.14.

IPP's knowledge is confined to events which occur in terrorist attacks. The database is organized so that MOPs for general categories of terrorism can be linked to more specialized MOPs which represent the location, target and agents of particular attacks. From these, IPP can make generalizations, such as that the Red Brigade usually operate in Italy, or that kidnaps often involve male

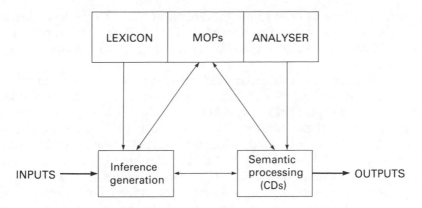

Figure 3.14   IPP modules

politicians and businessmen. When it is faced with a newspaper item, IPP activates its most 'interesting' terrorism MOPs and scans the story to see if the facts are similar to any of its generalized MOPs. If sufficient similarities are found, IPP uses these to produce a CD representation of the events in the story.

Like FRUMP, IPP is very good at using its MOP-based memory to select only the appropriate senses of words, e.g. that *sprayed* refers to bullets in *The gunman sprayed the street*. IPP also uses MOPs to generate possible interpretations for sentences. For example, on the basis of its knowledge of probable events in the 'kidnap' MOP, IPP might interpret a story about a gunman, a shooting incident and hostages as implying that the *gunman* is the Actor of *shoot* and *the hostages* the Object. This certainly speeds up decision making, but as a result programs like FRUMP and IPP tend to ignore 'uninteresting' words which may nevertheless provide important information about the structure of a sentence. Suppose the story had stated that *The gunman was shot by the hostages*. By failing to analyse words like *was* and *by* the program might mistakenly have gone for the more probable interpretation.

Riesbeck (1985) makes the point that part of the interest of these programs is to see how far it is possible to go in extracting meanings without paying attention to 'little' words. It is, of course, 'little' words like *by, have* and *to* which cause particular difficulty for parsing programs. This is because they can have so many meanings according to context, e.g. *I have to pass by the bakery to buy bread to take to my friend who wants to be taken to the park by Jane who has everything*. As a human reader you will probably not even have noticed all the different meanings of *have, by* and *to* in that sentence, but a computer parsing program has to be given precise

131

instructions about how to allocate each of them to the appropriate grammatical category. Programs like FRUMP and IPP represent a dedication to speed and plausibility at the expense of attention to syntactic detail.

One feature of IPP of particular interest to Schank is its ability to add new MOPs to its database. In the course of understanding stories, the program tests whether an incoming newspaper item is similar to any of its already stored MOPs. If the events are similar but not identical, IPP will produce an interpretation according to its present state of knowledge. But if it keeps meeting a set of events which don't quite match up, IPP can produce a new MOP to represent this information. For instance, faced with items about prominent women being kidnapped, IPP can set up a tentative new MOP separating out the particular details surrounding kidnaps of women from the kidnaps it already knows about. If enough female kidnaps occur, IPP adds a permanent MOP to its database. On the basis of this new information, IPP can produce a more accurate interpretation of stories, depending on whether they refer to kidnaps of men or women.

Such a system fits in well with Schank's notion of a dynamic memory. As IPP experiences events, it can make generalizations about actions which are common to many occasions, like waiting rooms, paying bills, or kidnaps, and derive new MOPs to represent these; in other words, it can learn from its experiences. Schank (1982b) stresses that language understanding and learning both depend on being 'reminded' of similar events in the past. All other programs we have discussed so far have had a static amount of knowledge put into their databases by the programmer. Like humans, IPP can extend its own database and so will interpret the same story differently depending on the current state of its knowledge.

In principle, of course, a program such as IPP will have to refer to an enormous number of MOPs if it is to model human memory and language. But it is difficult enough to specify how the program knows which terrorist MOPs are relevant to any particular story. Consequently, IPP is a program that has a great deal of in-depth knowledge within a very limited domain. IPP and FRUMP demonstrate very clearly the trade-off between deep knowledge of a few topics (IPP) versus broad sketchy knowledge of many topics (FRUMP), a dilemma that is familiar enough to humans.

4.6   The thread through Schank's work

I wouldn't be surprised if by now you are wondering what all these programs with appealing initials add up to. However there are some consistent principles running through the programs produced by the Yale AI research group under Schank's direction:

1 Analysis of sentences should be driven by the extraction of meanings, bypassing the need for a separate stage of syntactic processing. In fact, the programs try to ignore syntax as much as possible.
2 In order to understand a sentence, inferences have to be generated which go beyond the actual words in the sentence; for instance, *Mary punched Bill* implies that Bill was hurt.
3 Language understanding models need to incorporate some kind of inference program which sets up expectations. The semantic analyser is set to expect one meaning rather than another, thus reducing the problem of ambiguous words and sentences.

As a result of these three principles, one major problem for all the Yale programs is how to select from all possible inferences only those which are relevant to a particular interpretation. The inferential explosion arose out of the attempt to write computer programs which could produce sensible interpretations based on an understanding of the causes and results of events described in a text.

MARGIE analysed sentences into Conceptual Dependency representations on the basis of which inferences could be made. The problem was that there were so many potential inferences that it was difficult for the program to know which inferences to combine together in order to produce a representation for a whole text. The scripts in SAM were designed to provide a framework of causal chains to control inferences by restricting possible sequences of CDs to those that matched a script. However, scripts turned out to be *too* restrictive since stories often include bits and pieces from different scripts, and actions which deviate from stereotyped script routines.

The sketchy scripts in FRUMP were designed to get round the problem of too restrictive a sequence of actions by pitching scripts at the level of more general events, like 'police arrive at the scene'. Instead of having to match an exact sequence of actions involving the police marching or travelling in a coach to get there, many different sequences of actions could be accepted as indicating that the police were now present. Nevertheless, even sketchy scripts required that stories should follow certain sequences of events.

Finally, MOPs, as implemented in IPP, were developed to explain the fact that memories are organized on a more general basis than stereotyped script routines. The freedom this gives, though, leads right back in a full circle to the original problem of how to select from among a proliferation of possibly relevant MOPs. For this reason, MOP-based programs like IPP have had to restrict knowledge to a very limited domain.

Programs which generate knowledge-based expectations to direct semantic analysis also tend to run into the problem of how to take into account syntactic indicators and lexical meanings which do not fit in with these expectations. The advantage of ignoring many of the horrendous complexities of natural language grammars carries with it the disadvantage of finding only what you expect to find. It is, however, on the credit side of Schank's work that it has thrown up some of the really difficult issues in language understanding; in particular, the crucial problem of how to integrate linguistic knowledge of a particular language with appropriate general knowledge – scripts or MOPs – in order to produce semantic interpretations.

Summary of Section 4

- Schank and the Yale AI group have produced several language understanding programs, all of which use knowledge-based inferences to generate expectations about the semantic analysis of sentences.
- The basis of the MARGIE program was to generate inferences from CD representations of sentences, particularly inferences about all the possible causes and consequences of the events described. This led to an inferential explosion.
- The use of scripts in SAM and sketchy scripts in FRUMP was designed to control the selection of inferences by matching CD representations against causal chains of expected script events.
- Because script sequences proved too rigid, Schank proposed that knowledge is stored in the form of MOPs (Memory Organization Packets) which, as in the IPP program, can be called in to create superscripts for interpreting particular situations.
- The four programs MARGIE, SAM, FRUMP and IPP are compared in the chart opposite.

	MARGIE	SAM	FRUMP	IPP
DOMAIN	Sentences involving primitive Acts	Visits to restaurants and other script situations	Events which occur in newspaper stories	Terrorist acts
INPUT	Sentences	Stories and questions	Newspaper items	Newspaper items
OUTPUT	CD represent-ations	Paraphrases and answers	Interpret-ations	Interpretations
MODULES: Lexicon	Case frames for Acts	PP Memory including case frames, names	Case frames, word mean-ings, names	Case frames, word meanings, names
Semantic analyser	Analyser	ELI	Substantiator	Analyser
World knowledge	Inferencer	Scripts	Predictor	MOPs
PROCESSES	Inferences based on CD represent-ations	Matching CDs against causal chains of script events	Matching CDs against predicted events in sketchy scripts	Comparing CDs and MOPs and noting new generalizations
ADVAN-TAGES	CD case frame representations of sentences from which inferences can be made	Representations of script knowledge restricts inferences to sensible sequences of events	Really fast interpretat-ion of news items	MOPs can be used for interpretations and storing new information
DISADVAN-TAGES	A proliferation of unconnected inferences	Understanding restricted to rigid action sequences	Ignores a lot of syntactic and semantic information	MOPs can lead to a proliferation of inferences

5   *Some conclusions*

Part III has introduced a variety of Artificial Intelligence (AI) computer programs which have tried to model the extremely complex range of abilities involved in human language understanding. The summaries at the end of each section summarize the characteristic features and the advantages and disadvantages of each program. Figures 3.5, 3.7, 3.10, 3.12 and 3.14 show the relationship between the different modules in each language understanding program.

Perhaps the best way to remind you of the particular strengths and weaknesses of the programs discussed in Part III is to see how they might all cope with the same sample 'story':

>   *I hate my father. I shot my mother.*

For the purpose of this exercise, I shall assume that the database of each system has been updated with information about hating and shooting people. As you will see, this still leaves a lot of leeway in the methods used to store and process this information in order to produce the following outputs.

ELIZA:
WHY DO YOU HATE YOUR FATHER? TELL ME MORE ABOUT YOUR FAMILY.

BASEBALL:
Can only respond to queries in a specific format, e.g.
Whom do I hate? FATHER   *Who hates my father?* ME
Who shot my mother? ME   *Whom did I shoot?* MOTHER

SHRDLU:
Would start by parsing sentences as:
(NP pronoun *I*) (V *hate*) (NP *father*)
(NP pronoun *I*) (V *shot*) (NP *mother*)
In addition to answering questions like BASEBALL, SHRDLU has some knowledge about its own database. If asked *How do you know I shot my mother?* it could answer BECAUSE YOU TOLD ME SO.

MARGIE:

Actor: *Speaker*   Actor: *speaker*
Act: MTRANS   Act: PTRANS
Object: *hate*   Object: *trigger*
Direction TO: *father*   Direction TO: *forward*
      FROM: *speaker*   FROM: *back*
                          RESULT
                          Actor: *speaker*
                          Act: PROPEL
                          Object: *bullets*
                          Direction TO: *mother*
                                FROM: *gun*
                          RESULT
                          State: *dead*
                          Object: *mother*

SAM:

Same as MARGIE plus attempt to match against causal chains in hating/shooting script; so might report inconsistency between hating father and shooting mother.

FRUMP:

Actor: *speaker* (politician?)
Act: *insults*
Object: *father* (rival politician?)
        RESULT
Actor: *politician*
Act: *shoots*
Object: *wife of rival politician*

IPP:

Actor: *terrorist*
Act: PROPELS
Object: *bullets*
Direction TO: *hostage* (mother)
      FROM: *gun*
Note new MOP: Terrorists sometimes kill their mothers.

137

Having given you the flavour of each program's attempts to tackle a particular natural language input, I shall now turn to some general ways in which AI programs have sought to deal with the major problems of language understanding. Since no current computer program can even begin to match the human ability to talk about and understand a myriad of different topics, the decision for each program represents a trade-off between matching one aspect of human language at the expense of oversimplification of other linguistic abilities. For example, ELIZA and BASEBALL achieve their effects by operating at a 'shallow' level which only involves matching of prestored patterns in the database.

Various attempts have been made to deal with the deeper complexities of language understanding in a more flexible way. Some programs, like Winograd's SHRDLU, include a syntactic parser which is often of the type known as an Augmented Transition Network (ATN). While ATNs can call on semantic information to aid selection of syntactic categories, their aim is to produce a syntactic structure, which can form the basis for compiling a semantic interpretation. Such systems are known as syntactically driven parsers and are characterized as modular because they retain separate Syntax and Semantics modules.

In contrast, knowledge-based programs like Schank's generate inferences to guide semantic analysis of sentences directly on to meaningful representations. These systems, which are known as semantically driven parsers, bypass the need for separate Syntax and Semantics modules. Their main problem arises at the next level of semantic interpretations: that is, how to control the inferential explosion based on general knowledge. In MARGIE and SAM, the semantic analyser provides representations which trigger inferences to guide the selection of appropriate semantic representations. In FRUMP and IPP, general knowledge inferences come into operation right at the beginning with the result that the analyser sometimes overlooks potentially ambiguous syntactic constructions and word meanings altogether.

These two approaches represent a trade-off between painstaking linguistic analysis and relatively speedy general knowledge hunches. The interesting thing, though, is that all these types of program have had to restrict their domains in order to prevent a proliferation of possible word meanings and/or a proliferation of knowledge-based inferences. Restriction of vocabulary and possible topics helps to constrain the selection of sentence meanings *and* the selection of general knowledge schemas.

Currently, language understanding computer programs have diverged in two directions. Researchers, like Schank, who are still trying to model the general human ability to use language, have found themselves delving deeper into the way knowledge is organized in memory. The aim will be to retain the depth of knowledge of programs like IPP but to extend their scope to cover a much wider range of human knowledge.

In the other camp are researchers who are interested in developing natural language systems to enable human users to interact with computer programs which incorporate specialist knowledge. Such programs are often called *expert systems* because they are designed to provide expert help to humans. In these expert systems there is a large amount of information stored in the computer's database. What is required is a natural language *front end* so that the human user can ask questions in ordinary English without having to learn a complicated set of program commands. As computer expert knowledge systems are developed to cover such areas as medical diagnosis, legal advice, and travel information, it is obviously of great commercial importance to set up natural language front ends so that laymen can 'talk' to the computer. The aim would be to equip a knowledge system like BASEBALL with the plausible sounding conversational abilities of ELIZA.

Syntactic parsers like ATNs have proved useful for analysing passives and other grammatical constructions into syntactic structures which can be mapped on to knowledge representation formats in the database. In fact, Woods (1970) first developed ATN syntactic parsers to allow humans to interrogate his LUNAR program about information concerning the mineral composition of moon samples. The extreme difficulty of achieving language understanding front ends is demonstrated by the fact that most syntactic parsers only work for the particular knowledge databases for which they were designed. The basic difficulty seems to be that it is just as difficult to produce a purely syntactic 'knowledge-free' front end parser as it is to produce a 'syntax free' semantic interpreter.

You have probably noticed, too, that very little has been said about how the various programs are able to produce appropriate responses. It is difficult enough to try to specify how computer systems might represent inputs fed in by the investigator; it is even more difficult to program a system to decide in what form a meaning representation should be output. The problem is that there are so many possible ways of expressing the same thing. ELIZA is the best conversationalist because her replies are a mirror image of the sentences input by a human. Programs which generate 'deeper' semantic representations face the difficulty of choosing a surface representation to output as a complete sentence. Boden (1977)

139

quotes an amusing example when the response generator in the MARGIE system output a summary of the play *Othello* as 'Othello wanted to kill Desdemona by doing something because he heard from Iago Cassio had her handkerchief'. One feels that MARGIE would not have gone far as a playwright!

In all the models described in Part III, the apparent 'naturalness' of computer output is a bit of a cheat, being derived from a selection of pre-formed utterance patterns rather than from an ability to express whatever they want to say. As with language understanding, once again the main value of designing AI programs is the need to formulate precisely the representations and processing rules needed to comprehend and use language as humans do, thus disturbing any complacency cognitive psychologists may have had about understanding language.

Further reading

The ELIZA, BASEBALL, MARGIE and SAM programs are all described in Boden's book *Artificial Intelligence and Natural Man* (1977). This provides a very readable yet thorough introduction to AI models of human abilities.

Issues in Cognitive Modeling, edited by Aitkenhead and Slack (1985), includes several important articles which have been mentioned in Part III. 'What does it mean to understand language?' not only describes the original aims of the SHRDLU program but also shows how Winograd has extended his interests to other aspects of language understanding. An article by Riesbeck gives a nice short account of the FRUMP and IPP programs. The book also contains a paper by Schank in which he analyses the relationship between scripts and MOPs.

Another useful book of readings is *Strategies for Natural Language Processing*, edited by Lehnert and Ringle (1982). In addition to Waltz's 'state of the art' review of AI language understanding programs, there are several other interesting articles about attempts to model understanding of realistic language texts, including a longer account of the FRUMP system.

Overview

Because language is such a pervasive element in human behaviour, it is exceedingly difficult to divide language up into separate topics. So, as you have probably realized, the three parts of this book go over a lot of the same ground. Part I draws attention to the roll of different types of knowledge in language understanding. Part II considers how knowledge is involved in language processing, while Part III describes some attempts to incorporate knowledge and processes into computer models capable of understanding language. The three parts can be thought of as representing several 'passes' through the problem of explaining human language, gradually adding more depth on each pass.

It is equally difficult to separate language from other cognitive processes involved in thinking, remembering and acting. You may, indeed, have been wondering why a book on language understanding seems to concentrate as much on memory as on language understanding itself. This is because cognitive psychologists are interested in the question of how the competence to use a language is represented in memory. Their concern, though, is with language use in its widest communicative sense, thus blurring the traditional distinction between linguistic competence and performance.

In this Overview I will be presenting a cross-section of some of the main themes raised throughout the book in order to bring together aspects of language that were originally introduced in different sections.

1 Types of knowledge

A brief list of the knowledge available to language users would include at least the following:

1 The lexicon, i.e. rules for mapping sounds and written letters on to representations of word meanings. The question of whether these should be represented as lists of semantic features or as case frames was discussed in Part II, Section 2.
2 Syntactic rules, i.e. grammatical rules which specify how words should be combined. See Part II, Section 3, for a description of Chomsky's transformational grammar and the implementation of syntactic parsers as Augmented Transition Networks (ATNs).

3 Semantic rules, i.e. rules for combining individual word meanings into sentence interpretations. Section 2 of Part II introduced the problem of selecting appropriate word senses which was followed up in Section 4 by an account of a semantic analyser for extracting sentence representations.

4 Discourse rules, i.e. rules for combining sentence meanings into an interpretation of a whole text or conversation. This process depends on several different subsets of knowledge, including the way sentences relate to each other (see Part I, Section 3, on bridging inferences and Part II, Section 5.1, on local coherence rules); rules for extracting a macrostructure for a whole text (see the discussion of macrorules in Part II, Section 5.2); and knowledge about different types of discourse, e.g. story grammars (Part I, Section 4.5) and conversational rules for speech acts (Part I, Section 2.3).

5 General knowledge about the world, i.e. knowledge about objects and events, procedures and experiences. This type of knowledge is discussed throughout the book, notably in Part I, Section 4, and Part III, Section 4. In these sections the organization of world knowledge is described in terms of schemas, frames, scripts and MOPS. General knowledge schemas (MOPs) are derived from specific experiences of objects and events; they represent generalized expectations about the world as we experience it.

2   Inferences and context

All these different types of knowledge allow language users to make inferences about the probable meanings of what they hear and read. Part I, Section 3, was concerned with the role of inferences based on general knowledge. However, at all levels, it is assumed that knowledge generates expectations which guide language processing. For instance, the syntactic rules embodied in an ATN parser generate expectations about syntactic categories; semantic analysers generate expectations about conceptual cases; coherence rules allow people to make bridging inferences about what words refer to; scripts generate expectations about sequences of causally connected actions; story schemas generate expectations about goals and plans.

But why is all this inference-making necessary? Surely, if we can read the words in a language and are familiar with its grammar, we know enough to understand the language. One important theme of this book is that individual words and sentences are often ambiguous in isolation. Many examples were given of sentences which are potentially ambiguous, e.g. *Visiting aunts can be a nuisance, They are cooking apples, He gave her a ring, Put the green pyramid on the block in the box.* Yet, despite the ubiquity of ambiguity, when a sentence occurs in context, human language users scarcely ever notice that it could have more than one meaning; unconsciously they have made all sorts of inferences which lead them to select one interpretation rather than another. When we hear *Robin banks with Barclays* the possible interpretation of *banks* as a noun meaning river edges does not conform to expectations set up by the syntactic and semantic rules of English. The meaning of *He gave her a ring* will depend on the context in which we hear or read it, whether in a story about an engagement or in a context in which telephoning is the obvious topic.

It could be said that there is something of a paradox here. Instead of small linguistic units like words and phrases being easier to understand, it is actually easier to interpret whole sentences than individual words and to understand whole texts rather than single sentences. Words have many possible meanings, only some of which are appropriate in the context of a particular sentence. Potentially ambiguous sentences often have only one feasible sense in the context of a longer passage.

3   Language processing

While it is easy enough to demonstrate the facilitating effects of context, it is much more difficult to specify the precise processing operations we use for selecting one sentence interpretation rather than another. There are two basic approaches to modelling language processing. The first is that, at each level of analysis, possible sentence structures are generated for selection at the next stage. This implies a linear stage processing model of the kind shown in Figure 2.1. A second approach is that probable meanings are narrowed down by using information from several different sources, as in the heterarchical model in Figure 2.12. Within a heterarchical model there are many possible relations between syntax, semantics and world knowledge modules; these are charted in the computer models of language understanding discussed in Part III.

One general disagreement, first introduced in Part II, Section 4.4, is about whether a separate syntactic parser module is necessary. Winograd's SHRDLU incorporates a syntax module for analysing sentences, in contrast to programs like MARGIE and SAM which are semantically driven and dispense with syntax as a separate stage.

Schank's later models like FRUMP and IPP rely even more heavily on general knowledge schemas–sketchy scripts and MOPs–to select semantic interpretations.

The point was made at the end of Part III that language understanding models are faced with a dilemma: either to specify detailed rules for selecting syntactic categories and word meanings or to rely on world knowledge for resolving ambiguities. In the former case, there are too many sentence interpretations to choose from; in the latter, there is the danger of going for only the most probable interpretation. In either case, there is an explosion to deal with, making it difficult to select from many possible word senses and grammatical constructions or from a vast number of knowledge-based inferences. Designers of language models react by restricting knowledge databases to tiny domains: e.g. baseball games, toy blocks, script situations, newspaper items about terrorism.

4   Language as a psychological activity

So where does all this leave psychological theories of language? It seems obvious enough that linguistic knowledge must be stored in long-term memory and that linguistic processing goes on in some kind of short-term working memory. But do we, as Noam Chomsky suggests, have a separate linguistic competence? Or is our ability to use language part of our general ability to respond to the world about us? The experiments outlined in the various Techniques Boxes demonstrate that people can exploit all kinds of information in order to make inferences which aid understanding. Language does not occur in a vacuum but involves all our cognitive abilities and stored knowledge about the world.

As you might expect, human language users are normally more interested in the situations being described than in linguistic intricacies. When we are conversing in a language we know well, we seem to be speaking our thoughts directly, presenting the content of arguments rather than making linguistic decisions. The words on a page seem to 'speak' to us directly; the purpose of talking is to say what we mean. Yet this natural 'transparency' of language can be all too easily shattered when we attempt to express complex thoughts on paper. In these circumstances words and phrases seem to take on an obstinate life of their own.

The same is true when we try to learn another language. Despite all the general knowledge speakers may have in common, communication is very limited without a shared language. Acquiring a new language involves learning a whole linguistic system, including vocabulary, grammar, idioms and conversational conventions. As with other highly learned skills, once truly mastered, the whole linguistic apparatus seems to disappear, allowing us to concentrate on the interpretation of meanings and intentions. As they acquire competence, speakers move from the level of word meanings through sentence meanings to interpretations of discourses until they can use a language to communicate everything they want to say. It is at this stage, when language and meanings have become inextricably mixed, that it becomes impossible to distinguish the relative roles of language and thought. Do the particular languages we speak constrain the way we think or is language a neutral tool for expressing our thoughts?

As I concluded in Part II, Section 2.5, this is a complex issue. There are many concepts which seem to be universal to all human beings, e.g. semantic 'primitives' like 'cause', 'transfer of possession', 'move', 'ingest', and so on. Whatever the special customs of a society, its members are likely to want to talk about eating, giving, and moving. Schank's universal primitives are embedded in scripts which are particular to eating customs in American restaurants rather than to eating habits in all human societies. So language seems to depend both on universal knowledge shared by all human beings and on highly specific knowledge restricted to a particular society. All we can be sure of is that language simultaneously reflects and shapes our attitudes and actions within the society in which we live.

The exact relationship between linguistic skills, general knowledge and communication is mysterious indeed. At the same time as they have increased our understanding of language understanding, psychological investigations and computer models continue to reveal the incredible cognitive abilities and knowledge taken for granted by every language user. It is this multi-faceted nature of human language that guarantees it a central position in cognitive psychology.

Answers to SAQs

SAQ 1
(a) Most people would judge this to be an ungrammatical sentence according to the grammatical rules which define 'ideal' linguistic competence.
(b) In some conversational contexts the sentence could be a perfectly appropriate response, e.g. *Whose father is paying for the tickets?*

SAQ 2
(a) *Visiting aunts can be a nuisance* can either mean (i) that having to go and visit aunts can be a nuisance or (ii) that aunts who visit can be a nuisance.
(b) The Shivasi would assume meaning (ii), i.e. that aunts must be visiting them.
(c) Meaning (i) because the aunts could not visit them.

SAQ 3
(a) Given: Someone broke the window. New: It was Peter who did so.
(b) Given: Peter broke the window. New: He was kicking a ball around when he broke the window – with the strong implication that he kicked a ball through it.

SAQ 4
It has to be inferred that 'it' refers back to the two-mile run.

SAQ 5
Listeners to (a) would be more likely to assume that John had been using a hammer to 'pound' the nail.

SAQ 6
(a) Paris
(b) Yes
(c) One hour – as long as they don't quarrel!

SAQ 7
Most people assume after hearing the first two sentences that Mary is a little girl and so we are surprised to learn that she is old enough to have daughters. The default value for the age of someone buying ice-cream with birthday money is between about eight and twelve years old (at least mine is).

SAQ 8
(a) Customer: John
Restaurant: fast food type
Customer enters restaurant: John went in to fast food restaurant
Customer orders food: John orders hamburger
Food: disgusting hamburger
Tip: small
(b) An inference has to be made that customers tend to leave small tips if they are dissatisfied. Although the script does not specify this, knowledge about people's motives has to be available for understanding stories. At the very least the conclusion should be drawn that the disgusting food and the small tip are both deviations from the basic script and so are probably connected.

SAQ 9
There are many such inferences in the paraphrase, including the fact that John sat down, read the menu, ate the lobster, paid the bill and left the restaurant. All these are default values for events which are not mentioned in the story. The paraphrase is, of course, extremely boring, but the purpose of these inferences is to enable SAM to answer questions like *Who gave John the lobster?*

SAQ 10
Some actions which most of Bower *et al.*'s subjects agreed about include: wake up, get up, dress, eat breakfast, brush teeth, leave house.

SAQ 11
Story (b) requires the bridging inference that John fetched the *Good Food Guide* as part of a plan to look up a restaurant where he could eat.

SAQ 12
(a) Problem.
(b) Success.
(c) Mixed blessing.
(d) Perseverance.

SAQ 13
(a) Possible sentences would be *The violinist displayed a masterly use of his bow* and *At the end of the concert the violinist took a bow.*
(b) *Bank* can mean the edge of a river, a place for money transactions, an aeroplane turning.

SAQ 14
Possible synonym phrases might be: (a) *presented . . . . with*
                                           (b) *phoned*
                                           (c) *infected . . . . with*
                                           (d) *surrendered*
                                           (e) *resigned.*

SAQ 15
Bachelor (+ human) (+ adult) (+ male) (− married). One problem with semantic features is how to explain combinations like *bachelor girl, bachelor apartment*; or why it sounds rather odd to say *The Pope is a well-known bachelor*, although he is an adult male.

SAQ 16
(a) The subject of *admire* has to have the feature (+ human) so as to rule out *The stone admires John.*
(b) There are so many possible objects of *admire*, e.g. *I admire John, I admire jazz, I admire courage*, that it is difficult to know what selection restrictions are needed. Perhaps *admire* just needs the features: subject (+ human) and object (+ admirable).

SAQ 17
(a) Acceptable as meaning 'strike' because Peter is (+ human) and the object (rock) and instrument (ball) are both (+ physical object).
(b) Not acceptable, because the sense of *hit* meaning 'strike' requires (+ human) subject.

147

(c) Acceptable for 'collide', because Peter is (+ physical object) and so the rock (+ physical object) can 'collide' with him.

(d) Acceptable for both meanings of *hit*, because John is (+ human) for 'strike' but both John and Peter are (+ physical object) and so could 'collide'. However, I think you would agree that most people would assume the 'strike' sense, especially in the context of a dance!

SAQ 18
(a) Agent: *John*   Object: *window*   Instrument: *hammer*
(b) Instrument: *hammer*   Object: *window*
(c) Agent: *John*   Recipient: *Mary*   Location: *party*.
Note that there is an implied, but non-stated, Agent in (b), i.e. the person who used or threw the hammer, and a non-stated object in (c), probably either an invitation card or a verbal invitation.

SAQ 19
give (Agent, Object, Recipient)

SAQ 20
(a) ATRANS
(b) MTRANS
(c) PTRANS
(d) INGEST
(e) MOVE
(f) MBUILD

SAQ 21
> Actor: person
> Act: INGEST
> Object: edible or drinkable objects, or air
> Direction TO: inside person
>   FROM: outside person

SAQ 22
Other possible grammatical sentences are *Furiously sleep colourless green ideas* or *Green colourless ideas sleep furiously.*

SAQ 23

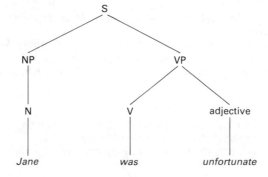

SAQ 24
(a)

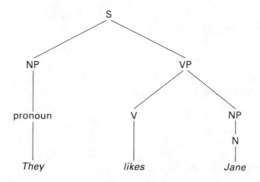

(b) You will have found that this grammatical sentence cannot be generated by the simple rules in Figure 2.4 because there is no rule which rewrites NP as an adjective on its own.

SAQ 25
Sentences (a) and (b) have similar deep structures representing the fact that a new student painted the picture. Sentences (b) and (c) have similar surface structures, i.e. the order of the words is much the same, but quite different deep structures. Sentence (c) has a deep structure indicating that someone painted a picture using a new technique.

SAQ 26
Sentence (a) should be the easiest because it is 'irreversible' according to our usual expectations of the doctor/patient relationships. Sentence (b) is considered to be 'reversible', although in our society there may be a slight expectation that a boy is more likely to kiss a girl than the other way round! Sentence (c) should take the longest because it contradicts our expectations. In fact, quite a few of Herriot's subjects misread it to mean that the lifeguard saved the bather.

SAQ 27
(a) (NP1) article *The* (NP2) N *boy* (NP3).
(b) (NP1) adjective *big* (NP2) adjective *blue* (NP2) N *blocks* (NP3).
(c) (NP1) pronoun *she* (NP3).
(d) There is no path through the NP network for this sentence. It could start off (NP1) article *The* (NP2) adjective *tall* (NP2) but from (NP2) there is no arc labelled with a word like *and*.

SAQ 28
(S1) find NP (NP1) skip (NP2) N *Jane* (NP3) NP finished (S2) find VP (VP1) V *was* (VP2) adjective *unfortunate* (VP3) VP finished (S3) sentence finished.

SAQ 29
　　Actor: *Jane*
　　Act: PROPEL
　　Object: *ball*
　　Direction TO: *through the window*
　　　　FROM: Jane's foot (implied)

Answers to SAQs

SAQ 30

(a)

(b)
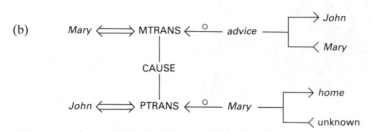

SAQ 31
Proposition–1: *said (teacher*, Proposition–2)
Proposition–2: *broke (John,window)*

SAQ 32
(a)
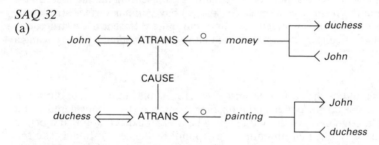

(b) Because both sentences have exactly the same CD semantic representation, Schank would predict that subjects would confuse the two sentences, just as they did in Johnson-Laird and Stevenson's (1970) experiment.

SAQ 33
Three possible differences are given below – you may have thought of others:
(a) SAM's answers are all relevant; ELIZA's replies range wider but are sometimes rather inconsequential, e.g. the reply to *Bullies*.
(b) ELIZA'S answers are mostly reflections back of the surface form of the questions; SAM's answers arise from his understanding of the (limited) restaurant script.
(c) In the SAM example the human asks the questions and the program answers; with ELIZA it is the program that interrogates the human.

SAQ 34
(a) Cleveland
(b) Winning scores: 5, 10
    Losing scores: 3, 2
(c) There is no information about this in the database.

SAQ 35
SHRDLU's outputs are more like SAM's than ELIZA's because they are based on an understanding of what is happening in the toy block world (just as SAM understands events in restaurants).

SAQ 36
(a) *John went down the road (in a bus).*
(b) *John went down (the road in a bus).*
Of course, humans would not even consider option (b) which implies that John was walking down a road which was in a bus. However, language understanding computer programs have to be given precise instructions about how to parse sentences like these.

SAQ 37
For the state of the blocks world in Figure 3.6 (a) the only interpretation which would make sense would be to place the green pyramid on the block which is already in the box i.e. interpretation (1). For state (b) the only sensible interpretation would be to move the green pyramid which is on the block and place it on the floor of the box i.e. interpretation (2).

SAQ 38
SHRDLU would say something like: I have to move the small green pyramid off the small red cube to somewhere else so that I can move the red cube. Next I will move the small blue pyramid out of the box to allow room to put the red cube on the floor of the box. Finally, I will place the red cube in the box and put the blue pyramid on top of it.

SAQ 39
(a) Possible inferences might include: Bill had done something to annoy John, John used his fist, Bill was probably hit in the face, Bill would like to get back at John.
(b) These inferences would be needed to interpret sentences like: *John was really annoyed, John's hand hurt more than Bill's cheek, How wise of John to leave before Bill regained consciousness.*

SAQ 40
(a) Actor: *John*

    Act: MOVE*

    Object: *fist*

    Direction TO: *Bill*

          FROM: *John*

*MOVE is the appropriate Act (rather than PROPEL) because it refers to moving a body part.
(b)

Answers to SAQs

SAQ 41

(a) The following actions in Figure 1.2 are not represented explicitly in Figure 3.9: Waitress gives food order to cook; Cook prepares food; Cook gives food to waitress. This brings home the point that it is always difficult to decide how many potential inferences should be built into knowledge representations.

(b)

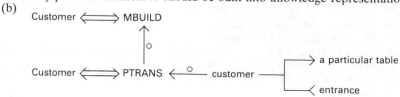

This CD represents the fact that the customer builds a mental representation (MBUILD) the object of which is the customer transferring (PTRANS) himself to a particular table.

SAQ 42

> Actor: demonstrators
>
> Act: PTRANS
>
> Object: demonstrators
>
> Direction TO: demonstration location
>
>   FROM: unknown

SAQ 43

Actions which would still be in the Doctor script would include: Talk to nurse, NURSE TESTS, and all the actions from Doctor enters to Get medicine. All the other actions would be part of more general memory representations, like checking in with receptionists, making appointments, and so on.

SAQ 44

The MOPs which would need to be changed include 'call plumber', 'professional home visit', 'arrive', and 'Plumber script', which includes the specific actions plumbers do. However, the main structure of MOPs about finding a professional to fix a problem, entering into a contract and being sent a bill would still be relevant; the only MOPs which would need to be added are specific details about the activities of lawyers as opposed to plumbers and the fact that one usually goes to visit a lawyer in his office.

References

AITKENHEAD, A.M. and SLACK, J.M. (1985) *Issues in Cognitive Modeling,* Lawrence Erlbaum (Cognitive Psychology Course Reader).

BARTLETT, F.C. (1932) *Remembering*, Cambridge, Cambridge University Press.

BLACK, J.B. and WILENSKY, R. (1979) 'An evaluation of story grammars', *Cognitive Science*, 3, pp. 213–29.

BODEN, M. (1977) *Artificial Intelligence and Natural Man,* Harvester Press.

BOWER, G.H., BLACK J.B. and TURNER, T.J. (1979) 'Scripts in text comprehension and memory', *Cognitive Psychology*, 11, pp. 177–220.

BRANSFORD, J.D., BARCLAY, J.R. and FRANKS, J.J. (1972) 'Sentence memory: a constructive versus interpretive approach' *Cognitive Psychology*, 3, pp. 193–209.

BRANSFORD, J.D. and JOHNSON, M.K. (1972) 'Contextual prerequisites for understanding: some investigations of comprehension and recall', *Journal of Verbal Learning and Verbal Behavior*, 11, pp. 717–26.

BRANSFORD, J.D. and JOHNSON, M.K. (1973) 'Considerations of some problems of comprehension' in W.G. Chase (ed.) *Visual Information Processing*, Academic Press.

BRANSFORD, J.D. and McCARRELL, N.S. (1977) 'A sketch of a cognitive approach to comprehension: some thoughts about understanding what it means to comprehend' in P.N. Johnson–Laird and P.C. Wason (eds) (1977).

CHOMSKY, N. (1957) *Syntactic structures*, Mouton.

CHOMSKY, N. (1965) *Aspects of the Theory of Syntax*, MIT press.

CHOMSKY, N. (1980) *Rules and Representations*, Blackwell.

CLARK, H.H. (1977) 'Bridging' in P.N. Johnson–Laird and P.C. Wason (eds) (1977).

CLARK, H.H. and CLARK, E. (1977) *Psychology and Language*, Harcourt Brace Janovich.

CLARK, H.H. and MURPHY, G.L. (1982) 'Audience design in meaning and reference' in J.F. Le Ny and W. Kintsch (eds) (1982).

COHEN, G. (1983) *The Psychology of Cognition*, Academic Press.

DE JONG, G. (1982) 'An overview of the FRUMP system' in W.G. Lehnert and M.H. Ringle (eds) (1982).

FILLMORE, C.J. (1968) 'The case for case' in E. Bach and R.T. Harms (eds) *Universals in Linguistic Theory*, Holt, Rinehart and Winston.

FOSS, D.J. and HAKES, D.T. (1978) *Psycholinguistics*, Holt, Rinehart and Winston.

GREEN, B.F., WOLF, A.K., CHOMSKY, C. and LAUGHERY, K. (1963) 'Baseball: an automatic question answerer' in E.A. Feigenbaum and J. Feldman (eds) *Computers and Thought*, McGraw-Hill.

GREENE, J. (1972) *Psycholinguistics: Chomsky and Psychology*, Penguin Books.

GREENE, J. (1975) *Thinking and Language*, Methuen.

HAVILAND, S.E. and CLARK, H.H. (1974) 'What's new? Acquiring new information as a process in comprehension', *Journal of Verbal Learning and Behavior*, 13, pp. 512–21.

References

HERRIOT, P. (1969) 'The comprehension of active and passive sentences as a function of pragmatic expectations', *Journal of Verbal Learning and Verbal Behavior*, 8, pp 166–69.

JOHNSON–LAIRD, P.N. (1974) 'Experimental psycholinguistics', *Annual Review of Psychology*, 25, pp. 135–60.

JOHNSON-LAIRD, P.N. and STEVENSON, R. (1970) 'Memory for syntax', *Nature*, 227, p. 412.

JOHNSON-LAIRD, P.N. and WASON, P.C. (eds) (1977) *Thinking: Readings in Cognitive Science*, Cambridge University Press.

KATZ, J.J. and FODOR, J.A. (1963) 'The structure of a semantic theory', *Language*, 39, pp. 170–210.

LE NY, J.F. and KINTSCH, W (eds) (1982) *Language and Comprehension*, North-Holland.

LEHNERT, W.G. (1981) 'Plot units and summarization', *Cognitive Science*, 4, pp. 239–331. (Reprinted in W.G. Lehnert and M.H. Ringle (eds) (1982).)

LEHNERT, W.G. and RINGLE, M.H. (eds) (1982) *Strategies for Natural Language Processing*, Lawrence Erlbaum.

MANDLER, J.M. (1982) 'Recent research on story grammars' in J.F. Le Ny and W. Kintsch (eds) (1982).

MANDLER, J.M. and JOHNSON, N.S. (1977) 'Remembrance of things parsed: story structure and recall', *Cognitive Psychology*, 9, pp. 111–51.

MILLER, G.A. and McKEAN, K.O. (1964) 'A chronometric study of some relations between sentences', *Quarterly Journal of Experimental Psychology*, 16, pp. 297–308.

MINSKY, M. (1977) 'Frame-system theory' in P.N. Johnson-Laird and P.C. Wason (eds) (1977).

PARSONS, D. (1969) *Funny Amusing and Funny Amazing*, Pan Books.

RIESBECK, C.K. (1985) 'Realistic language comprehension' in A.M. Aitkenhead and J.M. Slack (1985).

RITCHIE, G. and THOMPSON, H. (1984) in T. O'Shea and M. Eisenstadt *Artificial Intelligence: Tools, Techniques and Applications,* Harper and Row.

SCHANK, R.C. (1972) 'Conceptual dependency: a theory of natural language understanding', *Cognitive Psychology*, 3, pp. 552–631.

SCHANK, R.C. (1980) 'Language and memory', *Cognitive Science*, 4, pp. 243–84.

SCHANK, R.C. (1982a) *Reading and Understanding: Teaching from the Perspective of Artificial Intelligence*, Lawrence Erlbaum.

SCHANK, R.C. (1982b) *Dynamic Memory*, Cambridge University Press.

SCHANK, R.C. (1985) 'Reminding and memory organization' in Aitkenhead, A.M. and Slack, J.M. (1985).

SCHANK, R.C. and ABELSON, R.P. (1977a) 'Scripts, plans and knowledge' in P.N. Johnson-Laird and P.C. Wason (eds) (1977).

SCHANK, R.C. and ABELSON, R.P. (1977b) *Scripts, Plans, Goals and Understanding*, Lawrence Erlbaum.

SCHANK, R.C., LEBOWITZ, M. and BIRNBAUM, L. (1978) *Integrated Partial Parsing*, Computer Science Department, Yale University.

SEARLE, J. (1970) *Speech Acts*, Cambridge University Press.

SLOBIN, D. (1966) 'Grammatical transformations and sentence comprehension in childhood and adulthood', *Journal of Verbal Learning and Verbal Behavior,* 5, pp. 219–27.

THORNDYKE, P.W. (1977) 'Cognitive studies in comprehension and memory of narrative discourse', *Cognitive Psychology*, 9, pp. 77–110.

VAN DIJK, T.A. and KINTSCH, W. (1983) *Strategies of Discourse Comprehension*, Academic Press.

WEIZENBAUM, J. (1966) 'ELIZA – a computer program for the study of natural language', *Communications of the Association for Computing Machinery*, 9, pp. 36–45.

WHORF, B.L. (1956) *Language, Thought and Reality,* Wiley.

WINOGRAD, T. (1972) *Understanding Natural Language*, Academic Press.

WINOGRAD, T. (1985) 'What does it mean to understand language?' in A.M Aitkenhead and J.M. Slack (eds) (1985).

WOODS, W.A. (1970) 'Transition network grammars for natural language analysis', *Communications of the Association for Computing Machinery*, 13, p. 591.

Index of Authors

Index of Concepts

Index of Concepts